A Po
The L~~esson~~

for
"A Course in Miracles"

Mary Barbara Jankowski
Guided by Holy Spirit and Jesus

Before we begin, please know that I love you all and thank you for giving me the blessing of sharing my illuminations about the Course lessons with you. M.

Published by Mary Barbara Jankowski
Saint Petersburg, FL
Miraclescenter1@aol.com

Copyright © 2014 by Mary Barbara Jankowski
Miraclescenter1@aol.com

All rights reserved. No parts of this book may be reproduced or transmitted in any form or by any means, electronic or mechanical, including photocopying, recording, video, or by any information storage and retrieval system, without the prior written permission of the publisher. For information, contact Mary Barbara Jankowski.

A Path To Peace was first published in 2014

First Edition

ISBN 978-0-692-22128-0 Paperback

ACKOWLEDGEMENTS

All lesson titles, quotations and references from *A Course in Miracles* ("the Course") are from the "Foundation for Inner Peace" edition of *A Course in Miracles*.

I am forever grateful to Holy Spirit and Jesus for the Course. It has been a blessing in every area of my life.

Helen Schucman and Bill Thetford (the originators of the Course) deserve to be honored for their bravery and courage for scribing, at that time, the radical message of *A Course in Miracles*.

With the trust, love and support from all the members of the Course groups that I have facilitated throughout the years, the Course has *come to life* for me. For all of you, *my loves*, I am grateful.

Thank you to my family and friends for their loving encouragement. Thank you also to Irene Murphy, Nancy Wilson and Cathleen Schott for their assistance. A special thank you to Patti Jankowski for her final proofread of this book. Lastly, but certainly not least, I want to thank Terry Meachem for his dedication to the tasks necessary to transform my e-mails into this book and preparing it for publication. Without his tireless work, this material would not have reached you.

Illustrated by Cathleen Schott
mymiraclemuse.com

Cover Photo by Nancy Wilson
nancywilsonart.com

Love… Mary Barbara

AUTHOR'S PREFACE

Hello My Loves,

This book started as a daily e-mail to some of the members of the groups I facilitated. As the years went by, many people suggested that its message should be put into book form to accompany working with the lessons from *A Course in Miracles*.

I can only take partial credit for its message. The writing came through me at a time I was despondent in my spiritual life. I was downhearted with severe anxiety problems. I brought this about by avoiding dealing with several major life circumstances. I felt that I was at the lowest point in my spiritual life.

Nevertheless, I continued to do my daily Course lessons and in my meditations, after each lesson, this material was given to me. I was guided to write each day's message down. Later, it seemed right to e-mail this to members of our "Miracles" groups. It proved to be very helpful to this community. Today, our mailing list continues to grow. All things considered, this has been a natural progression of following guidance.

I truly believe, to loosely quote Mother Theresa, *that I was simply a pencil in the Hand of Jesus and the Holy Spirit.*

I sincerely hope that this material will be of benefit to you, in changing your thinking to a way that enhances your life on the path to becoming one of joy and peace as God intends for all of us.

Love and Light… Mary Barbara

"When you have learned how to decide WITH God, ALL decisions become as easy and as right as breathing. There is no effort, and you will be led as gently, as if you were being carried along a quiet path in summer." (ACIM)[1]

---

[1] T-14.IV.6

Lesson 1
"Nothing I see in this room (on this street, from this window, in this place) means anything."

And so we start with Lesson 1.

I would suggest that you apply the words of the first 40 lessons to anything in your life that is not peaceful. In this way, we will release the error thoughts of the past. For example, one might say, "Nothing I think about; money, another person, a health issue, etc., means anything". Use the lesson's title as thoughts come to mind throughout the day. Please follow this process with each of the lessons to come, and in this way, we release the past and allow God's Presence to reveal Itself to us.

Love and Vision to all.

Lesson 2
"I have given everything I see in this room (on this street, from this window, in this place) all the meaning that it has for me."

Please remember to apply this to any upsetting situation in your life.

We, through ego guidance, have given everything the meaning that is upsetting us. It is helpful to replace the word *see* with *think* or *perceive*. We are never upset by a fact.

Lesson 3
"I do not understand anything I see in this room (on this street, from this window, in this place)."

Again, let's remember to apply this to any upsetting situation in our lives.

The point of these lessons is to guide us to the realization that our thoughts do not mean anything unless they come from the Holy Spirit. Forgive me for repeating this so often, but these first lessons are the foundation for what the Course is teaching us.

First, the mind must be emptied so that the Light of Truth can shine through. Jesus is gently training us to be able to use this thought when something happens in our lives that has more significance than the things in this room. We might think, *I do not understand anything about this situation*, but the Holy Spirit does. Spirit guides us.

Through ego guidance, we do not understand anything about the upset. Ask Holy Spirit for guidance on what this truly means.

Remember, the Holy Spirit is your own right mind.

Lesson 4
"These thoughts do not mean anything. They are like the things I see in this room (on this street, from this window, in this place)."

The only thoughts that are real are the Thoughts of God.

The thoughts that are real are the ones we receive FROM God. Most of the time when, we are upset, it is not easy to hear the Thoughts of God. It is good to have a few favorite quotes from our Course to meditate on until we are back to peace. It is only when we are peaceful that we can truly hear the Voice of God.

Lesson 5
"I am never upset for the reason I think."

We are using this lesson to become conscious of how we allow our minds to wander.

Awareness is the purpose of this lesson. Awareness that we are NEVER upset for the current reason we think. We are always upset because of something from our past. Therefore, no matter what the situation, the call is for forgiveness

"The way to God is through forgiveness here. There is no other way." (ACIM)[2]

Lesson 6
"I am upset because I see something that is not there."

Remember, no one can do anything TO YOU.

The only reason we can be upset is the belief that something can separate us from the Love of God and that cannot be. All upsets are due to ego perception of the event.

Another important message in this lesson is that there are no *small upsets*. We are at peace or we are not at peace. When upset. get quiet and ask the Holy Spirit, which is our Right Mind, to reveal the Truth to you.

I like to pray thus: Father, reveal yourself to me in this.

---

[2] **W**orkbook-Lesson **256.** Paragraph**1**.Sentence**1**&**2**

Lesson 7
"I see only the past."

God is in the Now Moment.

Whenever we are upset, we have disconnected from the Thoughts of God by dwelling in the past or the future, which actually do not exist. Our minds can only connect with God in the Present Moment. The mind gets very upset when there is a disruption in the flow of Love from God to us. This is what is really, really upsetting us.

To try to *fix* an outer condition leads only to a temporary remedy. The ego will always find something else to tempt us with. Whenever upset, remind yourself of the following: *I am never upset for the reason I think. I am always upset because of something from my past.*

Give the upsetting thoughts to the Holy Spirit to heal. Let them go and move on.

Lesson 8
"My mind is preoccupied with past thoughts."

This lesson is a great threat to the ego mind.

The ego mind is the part of our mind that wants to keep the past alive and thus avoid the glorious *Now Moment* where God is present. Notice any resistance you may have as you practice. Remember, you do not have to like or understand these exercises. The suggestion is simply to take a few minutes to do them and the results will become evident in your consciousness.

When we blank out past thoughts, we leave space for the Thoughts of God to reveal themselves to us.

Lesson 9
"I see nothing as it is now."

The important point is not that we do not see the coat rack, etc., as it is now, but that we do not *see*, or perceive, anything in our human world as it is now. We see only the past, remember?

These lessons are guiding us to withdraw our dependence on the ego's use of the past and allow God to make each day new for us. WE are not our past!!! *"Behold, I make all things new for these words are true and faithful."* [3]

These thoughts are the road to attaining the consciousness of our True Identity.

Lesson 10
"My thoughts do not mean anything."

What a concept!!! My thoughts do not mean anything? How can this be?

Well, the implied idea is that *my ego thoughts do not mean anything, no matter how lofty they may seem.* Any thought that I think, apart from the Holy Spirit (my real mind), involves the illusion. These thoughts can be disrupted by something in the outer realm.

The only thoughts that have real meaning are the Thoughts of God. These are the thoughts that never change and only can give. As it tells us in the introduction to the Workbook, you don't have to like or understand this now, just practice this lesson.

The result will become evident as we progress.

---

[3] Revelation 21:5 Translations King James Version (KJV)

Lesson 11
"My meaningless thoughts are showing me a meaningless world."

This practice is particularly threatening to our ego mind.

The ego mind tells us that we know what everything means. It has taught us this from the beginning of the belief in time and space. Practicing calling our perceptions meaningless poses a real and powerful threat to the ego. Remember, the ego does not mean us well and the ego always lies.

Practicing this idea with neutral items in our world is a way to train our mind to use it when an upset is occurring. This lesson is showing us that nothing in this crazy illusion can hurt or injure us or make us permanently happy.

This is the good news and the bad news. Bad news since we have used our minds in such an ineffective way for so long, but good news since now God will take God's rightful place in our mind and permanent peace and joy will be the result.

When the ego's madness has been erased from our minds, the Power and Glory and Love, which is our natural inheritance from Almighty God, will be evident to us forever more. When we think about it this way, practicing this lesson seems like such a little thing to ask. Remember, God will take the last step in our remembering.

Practice this lesson often. It is a major step to our freedom.

Lesson 12
"I am upset because I see a meaningless world."

What a wonderful gift this lesson brings to us.

It is such a relief (except to the ego mind) to be reminded that in

Truth everything in this dream world is meaningless. The ego does not want to accept this, but searches through the past for a meaning that will frighten us. Once this meaning is presented to us and we accept it, it seems real to us.

For me, I am glad to know that this world is actually as meaningless as it seems. Nothing here is consistently peaceful and loving.

Let's take the leap now and allow our minds to let go of all the things we think we know and allow God's Voice to be our authority. If you find yourself in a state of mind where God's Voice seems obscure, use the lesson titles or other Truth statements as the thoughts you hold in your holy mind.

Another solution is to join with someone whom you know will hold the Truth for you. This will be the doorway through which God's Word will enter. Our lessons promise that we will experience the *indescribable happiness* that is God's Will for us.

Suggestion: As you probably realize, I only quote a portion of the lesson. Please read the whole lesson as written by Jesus.

Lesson 13
"A meaningless world engenders fear."

This lesson is about our fear of letting go of control.

However, it is control that we do not really want. We think that we feel more confident thinking that we know what things mean, even if the meanings we give are fearful and faulty. Of course, we are neither consistently peaceful nor joyful.

To allow ourselves to realize that we must live moment-to-moment, trusting in the Loving Arms of God, can be terrifying to us if we are valuing something here in the illusion. It frightens us because we think we are in competition with God about our peace and happiness. If we were to change the name of God to Joy, Peace, Love, Abundance, Wholeness, Beauty and Freedom; perhaps it would be easier to let go of our need to be in control, and give up thinking we are competing with God concerning what things mean.

We want to be happy. *"God's Will for us is perfect happiness,"* (ACIM)[4] NOW. Let's go forward with this thought to guide us. To anything that comes into our mind say:

This is meaningless; God's Will is done, everyone is happy-- Thank you, God.

Lesson 14
"God did not create a meaningless world."

*These lessons about **meaninglessness** can be confusing and very threatening to the ego.*

When we say *meaningless,* we do not mean that thoughts do not have effects in the ego world. We are saying that ego thoughts are not in the Mind of God, so they are without lasting effects. It is the body sensations that tell us what is meaningful to us and what is not. The Course teaches the physical body, in Truth, is not real. It is an expression of the belief in separation from God's Love.

If we remembered our True Identity as a Spirit of God, nothing here would be meaningful except that which reflects the visibility and tangibility of God. As we take our power away from the world of illusion, it will disappear into the nothingness from which it came.

I know this is hard to believe when we are in the middle of *issues* in our lives, but let's keep in mind all the times that we turned to Truth and then the *issue* disappeared.

Let's spend our time strengthening our Trust in the Truth and let the meaningless ego thoughts from the past be forgotten.

---

[4] W-100.2.1

Lesson 15
"My thoughts are images I have made."

Again, we are being led to withdraw our interpretations from the world we think we see.

Until we let go of the belief that we know what everything is, we cannot experience God's World. What we are seeing now comes from past experiences. All the images we see with our ego mind vacillate between good and evil, depending on our interpretations. These interpretations are simply images we are bringing from what we call the *past*. Just ask several people to describe a shared event.

Our Course will take us back to the place where God's Mind is the only Mind we know. It is so comforting to know that this is inevitable.

Let's remember that God's Mind came first and filled all there is. And it is good, very, very good.

Lesson 16
"I have no neutral thoughts."

These beginning exercises are focused on helping us become aware of not only what we are thinking, but also of the effects our thoughts have on our lives.

Fear thoughts, although unreal, create the world we see, just as thoughts of Love allow God's World to be revealed. It does not take much effort to look at the current situation in the world to realize the amount of fear that people are holding in their minds.

We have our dear Course to help us become the Bringers of Light to this tired old world. It does not take a majority of us to have an effect because Truth is with us. Allow yourself to know the importance of what we are doing. We are moving toward the Great Awakening and those who are aware will be the ones to bring this about.

Ask Holy Spirit to reveal to you the fear thoughts you are hiding in your mind, and then say the forgiveness prayer (below). In this way, you will restore the power of your mind to its rightful place, and the Peace of God will become more and more evident.

FORGIVENESS PRAYER (to be used when upset):

Holy Spirit, whatever this represents, I give it to you to forgive and heal for me. Take it from me and heal it for me. Don't let me hurt myself with this anymore. Behind this is a miracle to which I am entitled, and I joyously accept that miracle now. Thank you, Spirit. Amen

Lesson 17
"I see no neutral things."

Again, we are asked to realize the power of our thoughts. We are One with God and therefore there is no limit to the power we possess. We are being asked to become aware of our thoughts and then to realize that this is what shows up in our lives. It is because a thought does not usually materialize immediately (because of our belief in time) that we do not realize that the world we see is the product of our thoughts.

What we are seeing in our world today is yesterday's thoughts. This is the good news and bad news. The bad news is that we would send these experiences to ourselves. Hence, the good news is that since we are the sender, we can now stop. Know that any fearful thoughts you are entertaining at this time can be changed.

As we begin to love ourselves more and more, we will become vigilant about the thoughts that we allow to dwell in our holy minds.

I would like to suggest the following thought to occupy your mind today and then watch for the results in your life.

"I can do all things through God, Who strengthens me." [5]

---

[5] Philippians 4:13 New King James Version

Lesson 18
"I am not alone in experiencing the effects of my seeing."

Let's review a message from a previous lesson.

What we think within is shown to us without. One has only to watch TV or read the newspapers to see how ideas spread. Once these stories are presented to the public, they are thought about and believed and repeated. Let us be the ones to turn this around. We can be the ministers of God who live the message of *A Course in Miracles* and other high paths.

Since we are not alone in experiencing the effects of our seeing the world, let's be sure that we see the world through the eyes of Love. In this way, we can become the Highest examples of Peace and Love for others to follow. We will not be alone in its effects.

Let there be peace on earth and let it begin with me and my thinking.

Lesson 19
"I am not alone in experiencing the effects of my thoughts."

At first this lesson does not seem to be different from yesterday.

When the Course uses the word *see*, it is referring to *perception*. Obviously, thoughts and perceptions go together, but today's lesson is bringing us back to the originator of the perception. How does it feel to know that there are no *private thoughts* or private perceptions? It would seem that this is not true. We cannot read each other's minds, or can we?

If we are really honest with ourselves, we must admit that we can tell what others are thinking about us and about the world without a word being said. Reach down into your heart and think of someone and *feel* if you know what he or she really thinks about you. Then realize that they can do the same about you and your thinking. If we truly believe this, we should be very vigilant about what we think about each other.

Well, let us live our lives as if this were true. Our Course is telling us that this is the truth. If you notice that you are entertaining judgmental thoughts about a person, train your mind to think the word Love, Love, Love, over and over. This will keep our minds turned to Truth and Holy Spirit will do the rest.

Try this for a period of time and see if your relationships, health and state of mind improve. This is Gods' Will and ours.

Lesson 20
"I am determined to see."

This is an intriguing lesson.

It is asking us to practice something trusting that will lead us to peace. This lesson is asking us to become more and more aware of what we are thinking. It does not yet tell us what we are *determined to see*, but it is asking us to just be willing to practice the idea.

The main wisdom to draw from this lesson is that we yearn to be peaceful and happy all of the time. This is ours by Divine Right, but we really don't know how to accomplish this. One example of this is that we actually are convinced that thinking we are RIGHT about some seeming injustice will make us happy. What a crazy mad idea! But we continue to ruminate about this. We believe that more and more thinking will bring us the happiness and peace we really want.

The following is one of my favorite quotes. It is from Lesson 248. *"I have disowned the truth. Now let me be as faithful in disowning falsity."* (ACIM) [6]

Holy Spirit, today we are determined to see. Thank you.

---

[6] W-248.1

Lesson 21
"I am determined to see things differently."

Notice what arises when you ponder the thought that "a slight twinge of annoyance is nothing but a veil over intense fury".

Interesting, yes? I have tested this out and found the truth in this statement. Something happens that we do not like and we like to tell ourselves *this is not that bad*. But if we honestly go deep within ourselves we would find that it IS that bad, to us.

It is important that we become aware of how we are blocking God's Love. As we go along releasing these blocks by admitting to ourselves the truth about our emotions, we can ask Holy Spirit to forgive and heal them for us and move on. In this way we become willing to see things differently. This becomes so much easier as we practice this idea. The results will help us to make this a part of our daily lives.

Remember Heaven awaits but our acceptance.

Lesson 22
"What I see is a form of vengeance."

I am sure we have all noticed that when we are upset and angry about something in our lives, this colors how we see everyone and everything.

When we are in a joyous place this is how we see the world. This lesson reminds us that if fear and attack is the energy in our mind that we see with, then this is what will color our world.

As we fill our minds with the Thoughts of God, we will see the world as simply a visible reflection of Love and Peace. Let us stop believing in the power of anything not of God to affect us. When we are having an experience of fear, know that we are seeing through the lens of attack and counter attack. The solution is simple; ask yourself from whom am I withholding Love?

Remember our saying, the only pain we can experience is from the thought that now I can't love you.

Lesson 23
"I can escape from the world I see by giving up attack thoughts."

How simple this lesson makes it all seem. And it is simple indeed.

We have become so unconscious of what attack thoughts actually are, that we continue to hurt ourselves with them. By now, most of us know that judgmental thoughts, about another or ourselves, are attack thoughts. But it is more veiled to realize that our thoughts of the *sins of others against us,* are also attack thoughts. When this is brought to our attention, we can see how thinking either way robs our peace of mind.

Further, do we realize that the long list of things that we declare *good for us* and *not good for us,* are also attack thoughts? We make up this list and then punish ourselves when we do not comply with it. How funny this would be if it did not have such ramifications.

The ego tells us that if we were to give up thinking as we do, all would be chaos. However, Holy Spirit assures us all would be God. Let's spend today just becoming aware of all that we judge today and know that these are attack thoughts. Then, we invite Holy Spirit into these thoughts.

In this way, we allow the Thoughts of God to become the only ones that occupy our holy minds.

Lesson 24
"I do not perceive my own best interests."

Of course, we know our own best interest. It is to search the world for that which will bring us the peace and happiness we desire. However, one must remember that the ego's dictum is, *seek and never find.* This lesson reminds us, as long as we think we know our own best interest, Holy Spirit cannot bring us the gift we really seek. That gift can only be obtained by "*But seek ye first the kingdom of God, and His righteousness; and all these things shall be added unto you,"* [7] or as I have been using-- The Kingdom of Now. I also like to remember the words from the Bible that say, *"in the beginning, God."*

How many times have we thought we knew our own best interests, only to obtain what we desire and have it either be very unfulfilling or have it come with the "gift" of fear of loss?

The simple and often stated concept for us to remember is to trust Holy Spirit to guide us to what we truly desire. Whenever you feel a desire in your heart know that, first of all, what you truly want is the Love of God. You have lost touch with the fact that you always are One with the Love of God.

Then, gently and without much energy, say to yourself often, *Thank you God for the perfect outcome*. I like to be more specific and say, *Thank you God for my perfect job, home, car etc*. This releases us from the desperation for these things because we already have what we really, really want and that is the Love of God.

Lesson 25
"I do not know what anything is for."

These beginning lessons can often seem to be quite strange.

We must trust that the Course knows what it is doing and that it is leading us to a higher consciousness of what we are and what the world is for. It may seem very odd to look at the familiar things in our world and say we do not know what they are for.

We are walking a very gentle path. It is taking us from recognizing this principle about neutral objects, which have little emotional impact for us, to helping us apply it to experiences which we think have great importance. The Course teaches the following that I always find helpful: Forget not that the healing of your mind is all the world is for.

It takes training and willingness for us to surrender to this Truth.

---

[7] Matthew 6:33 King James Version

Lesson 26
"My attack thoughts are attacking my invulnerability."

One of the most important lines in this lesson is the one teaching us that the effect of attack thoughts weakens us IN OUR OWN EYES.

The ego reminds us that when someone seems to be attacking us, this makes us feel vulnerable. We think that attacking in return will weaken our enemy. How foolish is this system of belief. Little do we realize that we can be attacked only by our own thoughts, and so can the person we may wish to attack.

We live in a world of ideas. There is nothing out there that can hurt or injure us unless we give it permission to. We have an old saying, *I am never upset by what you say to me. I am ALWAYS upset by what I say to me, about what you say to me.* Well, this is true for all of us-- the so-called giver and so-called receiver of an attack.

Another little hint that helps when dealing with attack thoughts is to take the *to me* from our perception of the situation. No one is doing anything *to me*. I am doing it all *to me* by my perception of what is done. Nothing can change what I am. I am the Child of God, whole and complete and full of joy.

This is how I was created and thankfully this is how I remain no matter what.

Lesson 27
"Above all else I want to see."

*This lesson is an important one. It is leading us to equate **seeing** with **vision**.*

We have learned *vision* is seeing through the eyes of the Holy Spirit. This lesson asks us to become willing to give up the control that we think we may have in a situation and allow Holy Spirit to be our only guide. This will become more comfortable as we remind ourselves that in our Course, the Holy Spirit is called the "Spirit of Joy". (ACIM)[8]

Lesson 28
"Above all else I want to see things differently."

This lesson has far-reaching effects on our peace of mind.

It gives us a practice to use with everything in our lives, especially those things that rob our peace. We think that we know what everything means. We think we know its purpose. However, as we talked about before, the purpose of everything here is to lead us back to the Awareness of Love's Presence.

We are being led to understand that everything we see in the so-called *outer world* is an image we have made. We are living in a world of ideas. When we withdraw our ego meanings from everything, the Kingdom of God will be revealed again to us. Everything is the visibility and tangibility of God. All is to remind us of our Oneness with God. But first, one must release the thought that there is only one way to see the world.

*This may start with the **little** upsets in our lives, but will eventually lead us gently and lovingly to the Great Awakening.*

Lesson 29
"God is in everything I see."

The practice of this lesson on a daily basis will make all our days peaceful and joyful.

If we were willing to give up our perception of the world and let

---

[8] T-5.II.2. 1

the Holy Spirit guide us, we would know joy beyond compare. God is in everything I see because there is only God. There is only Oneness, no matter how we have tried to break up the Oneness into little separate expressions. Remember, God came first and filled all there is. This is why God is in everything I see. It is just that sometimes we do not see clearly, but through a glass darkly. Let us rejoice and be glad that God is in everything we see.

How safe it makes one feel to know that we are in the Arms of our Heavenly Father, safe and healed and whole.

Lesson 30
"God is in everything I see because God is in my mind."

How happy our world will be to us when we truly get the message of this lesson!

God is in everything I see. How could we not feel joyous and safe if all we perceive in the world is peace and love and joy and abundance and wholeness and freedom and beauty? These are some of the attributes that our Course ascribes to God. This is all we will ultimately perceive as we look around our world, near and far, no matter what the appearance. We remind ourselves that God is here because God is in our Mind. Our only true desire is to remember God. This is our heart's desire and this lesson teaches us how to train our minds so that God is all we see, all we can ever see.

God is ALL there is.

Lesson 31
"I am not a victim of the world I see."

Either we are the victims of the outer world or we are not. It is up to us to use our free will to choose what the truth is for us. It is so much a part of the illusionary world to blame something or someone for our state of mind. We think surely, if *this* were different, it would be easier for me to be peaceful and happy. Most of us have lived long enough to know that something else always comes along to tempt us to think, *when this is resolved, then I will be happy*, and on and on.

Let's wake up. There is nothing out there. It is all going on in our Holy Minds. We are making it up and then believing it. The practice of this lesson as a regular part of our thinking will bring us to the awareness of what we are doing to ourselves. Let's stop hurting ourselves with ego lies. There is nothing that can change that we are as God created us. However, because of our belief in separation, we can live as though this is not the Truth.

To quote a portion of one of our favorite lessons, *"At first to be but said and then repeated many times; and next to be accepted as but partly true, with many reservations. Then to be considered seriously more and more, and finally accepted as the truth."* (ACIM)[9]

Let's start with knowing that there is no power in fear. We can only be victims of our own thinking. This may seem uncomfortable at first. However, as we say/think it more and more often, it will become as natural to us as the ego way of thinking had previously become. *Let the following be our daily affirmation:*

I AM AS GOD CREATED ME, A POWERFUL SPIRITUAL BEING GUIDED BY WISDOM AND LOVE.

Lesson 32
"I have invented the world I see."

At first this idea seems too incredulous to believe.

How could I have invented the situations I don't enjoy when I seem to want so badly to eliminate them? Well, herein lies the relief. We have missed the first step. We have not allowed

---

[9] W-284.1.5&6

ourselves to own the fact that we are the inventor of every situation in our lives (the so called good and so called bad). It is in this one fact that our freedom lies.

If we will just be a little willing to accept that we have invented all situations as we see them, then the key to our escape will be placed in our hand. This is not God's World. This is the world of imagination made by beings that have forgotten Who they truly are. Do you not know ye are Gods?

As we practice today's idea, the realization that we are the authors of this world will become more and more evident. In this realization, we will become aware that the problem lies not in God's willingness to help us.

It lies in our own willingness to be healed and whole as we were created.

Lesson 33
"There is another way of looking at the world."

It must be quite obvious that these lessons are meant to jar us from our preconceived notions of the world.

Most of these opinions and judgments are not even our own. They were taught to us, essentially unconsciously, by the world in which we seem to inhabit.

Jesus is taking us gently, as always, but firmly, into awareness. He takes us first to the realization that it is our thoughts that are the cause of everything and then into realizing that "*there is another way of looking at this world*". What an insult to the ego who screams in our minds, "No, no, there is only one way of looking at the world and that is my way!" We mistakenly accept ego thinking as our own thoughts.

So, dear ones, let's be brave and practice today being aware of our thoughts using today's idea. There IS ANOTHER WAY, a better way; the Holy Spirit's way of looking at this situation.

Thus we remove the blocks to the awareness of the Flow of God's Love.

Lesson 34
"I could see peace instead of this."

How simple it is to have peace of mind.

Let go of what we do not want and hold in our mind what we do want. It is by our free will that we have this power. Yet, in this ego world, not many of us realize that this choice is available to us. Oh, we know this when we are in a high space and feeling our Oneness with God. But when something occurs and we have attached an ego meaning, it becomes more difficult to choose peace. The ego tells us that somehow choosing peace, at these times, will be a loss to us. This would be funny if the consequences were not so great.

It takes the practice, which the lessons prescribe, to give our minds the muscle to know quickly when we are out of peace and then to make the choice for the Peace of God. It is by the use of this practice and others that we find ourselves living in the wonderful Now of peace and love and joy as God intends.

As the Bible shares with us, *"Let not your heart be troubled; neither let it be afraid."*

Lesson 35
"My mind is part of God's. I am very holy."

As I practice this lesson, I realize that all the things I thought I saw about myself are coming from a lower level of mind.

It is from this level (the ego based level) that I establish a false identity and then surround myself with that which would prove I am right about this identity. Then, as I add the words from the title of today's lesson, I sense the level of my thinking rise to a higher and more peaceful level. It is quite an experience. Please practice this with as much awareness as you can. This is bringing us to the point of trust and surrender that is necessary to let the outer world go and accept ourselves as the One God created. We were created in holiness and it is in holiness that we remain, *Nothing* can change this.

Lesson 36
"My holiness envelops everything I see."

Our lessons lead us ever so gently back to the Garden of Eden.

Once we realize that our minds are holy, because they are part of God's Mind, we begin to remember our original state of mind. This is One with our Creator and all the Created. If our minds are holy, so must everything we see also be holy. Holiness cannot perceive sin. Not only does this lesson help us to live in a different frame of mind than the one the ego dictates, but it reminds us that everything God *sees* must be very holy too.

There is nothing we can do that would change God's view of us. Guilt is a ridiculous idea of the ego. There is no sin and there is no guilt because God cannot perceive this and what God sees is Real.

In this way, we let God's Love engulf us and innocence prevails.

Lesson 37
"My holiness blesses the world."

With holiness comes the awareness of God's Love.

How could the world *not* be blessed by us? When we see everyone and everything through the eyes of love and holiness, then Judgment becomes impossible. Defenses of any kind are unnecessary.

Recall how it feels to be in the presence of someone who you know is not judging you. How easy it is at these times to feel your own holiness and to bring this awareness to others as you go through your day. It is God's Will that we know our holiness. Anything else is simply error thought. With holiness comes all the blessings of God. *"But seek ye first the kingdom of God, and his righteousness; and all these things shall be added unto you."* [10]

How safe, how peaceful and how happy the world becomes when we are aware of our innocence and see only this in others.

Lesson 38
"There is nothing my holiness cannot do."

This lesson is again reminding us of our Oneness with our Heavenly Father.

"There is nothing my holiness cannot do because the power of God lies in it." If we could just accept this totally, there would be no sorrow or pain that could change the vibration of our mind. What could possibly disturb the calm peace of God's mind!!!

Perhaps it will help us to understand the magnitude of this message if we turned it around. We remind ourselves that there is no good that our belief in guilt cannot block. Our holiness is the acceptance of ourselves as God created us. Our feeling of guilt is the rejection of this Truth. Nothing we do, or anyone else does, can change Eternal Love and Innocence.

In this Eternal Love and Oneness lies all the Power and Glory of God. What miniscule belief or situation can stand up to this? *"And we know that all things work together for good to them that love God, to them who are the called according to His purpose."* [11] We are accepting this when we recognize our Identity as established by God.

In this recognition only the Kingdom of God is experienced once more.

---

[10] Matthew 6:33 King James Version
[11] Romans 8:28 King James Version

Lesson 39
"My holiness is my salvation."

Who can dispute that guilt is hell?

We would just have to think of a time when we felt guilty to know the answer. How wonderful to know that the guilt is coming from the ego thought system and is thus totally insane. Guilt is not from God and can easily be disregarded. Most of us have somehow learned that God is the giver of guilt when we have done something that is against His *perceived laws,* and that some sort of suffering is the payment. When we really look at this it becomes apparent how ridiculous this is.

How can Holiness give guilt? Guilt is unholy! God can only give what It possesses. What we are calling guilt is merely having unloving thoughts. We were created to Love and when we are not in this vibration there is a feeling felt that is hell. The ego keeps this fact hidden from our minds because if we realized that the problem was simply that we forgot to love, we would remedy it at once.

From now on let us remember that any time we are not in peace, it is because we have chosen not to love. The process probably went something like this. Someone or something did not fulfill the function we had assigned to it. We tell ourselves, *Now, I can't love you.* Little do we realize that with this thought we condemn ourselves to the hell of guilt. Remember, *God is but Love, and therefore so am I.*

With this thought we are aligned with God once more and guilt is gone and peace and goodness are ours once again.

Lesson 40
"I am blessed as a Son of God."

This Lesson asks us to remind ourselves again and again of what we truly are and what we are ENTITLED to as God's Creation.

How we have talked ourselves out of our Entitlement!!! WOW! Please meditate on the fact that we are as God created us, *not* what we have made of ourselves. God can only create Goodness. It might be helpful to write this out on several index cards and place them throughout your home. It is God's Will that we accept our rightful place in Creation. It is up to us to be willing to do so. *"I am blessed as a Son of God"*... and I am entitled to all that the Kingdom of God offers.

There is nothing we have to do but accept this, and it will be true for us, NOW!

Lesson 41
"God goes with me wherever I go."

First of all, I would like to recommend that you read this lesson in the Workbook. It is such an important and comforting teaching.

How peaceful it is to know that we are never alone, no matter how the ego interprets our circumstances. When we really have the experience of God's Presence, there is nothing that can take away the sense of peace and belonging that we feel. Of course, God goes with us-- there *IS* only God! There is not one place or time where God is not. It is only by listening to the ego's harsh voice that we could think that we are alone and must handle life's events on our own.

We well know that the ego's advice is to *fix* the outer world and then we will feel the peace and belonging for which we so yearn. But we all know from many, many experiences that this does not work on a permanent basis. The only cure is solving the real problem, which is the belief that we can be separate from *All There Is*. It takes practice to finally come to the realization that *wherever I am, God is*. And where God is, there is peace and love and joy.

It is truly worth the discipline that the lesson asks, to heal our sense of separation and return our ego minds to the Mind of God.

Lesson 42
"God is my Strength. Vision is His gift."

We can see how the two thoughts in the title of this lesson go together.

Let us remember that Vision, as the Course uses it, is seeing through the eyes of the Holy Spirit, or seeing truly. God is our Strength, not our own puny strength, and with this acceptance Vision comes naturally to us. If we can give up the thought that we are alone and must handle life by ourselves we will experience the strength of God, which is ours by Divine Right. As a result of accepting help from our Heavenly Father, Vision will be the result.

We know how it feels to experience things through the eyes of the Holy Spirit. There is a completely different effect when we tune in to Spirit's Guidance. As this lesson tells us, "*You cannot but be in the right place at the right time. Such is the strength of God. Such are His gifts.*" So wherever we are right now and whatever is happening, is happening for us, not *to us*. We are right where we are meant to be.

We are where we are to heal our minds so that we can accept what is ours and live in the glorious Joy and Peace of our Creator once more.

Lesson 43
"God is my Source. I cannot see apart from Him."

This lesson, as do all the lessons, has as its purpose the restoration of the memory of God.

We have made a way of seeing the world that has excluded Our Creator. However, God has given us the bridge to bring us back to His Awareness. Perception can easily be called an interpretation. This interpretation usually comes from the ego thought system. Thus, one can forgive someone we love for a certain deed and judge someone we do not like differently for the same deed. We do this because we think we *understand* the friend. However, this form of *understanding* is simply a way to keep ourselves and others separate.

When we give our Mind and all of its thinking to the Holy Spirit, we will see everyone with the *eyes* of God, which is called knowledge. In this view, we will see all as coming from the same Source as we do. We will not let appearances fool us into making some people special and others worthy of our judgment. The very logic that we have used to foster our belief in separation, when used by the Holy Spirit, will heal our minds and bring God back to Its rightful place in our Mind.

Lesson 44
"God is the Light in which I see."

Again, I would like to recommend that we read the lessons in their entirety in the Workbook and practice as advised. The lessons are becoming much deeper and there is so much more substance there for us. Just think about it.

If you could stand aside from the ego by ever so little, you will have no difficulty in recognizing that its opposition and its fears are meaningless. I have found several effective ways of doing this. The one I would like to recommend is writing out the issue that is concerning you. Then, go to the index of the Workbook and write out and apply the title of each of the first 40 lessons for this topic.

For example: Nothing I see, or think, about this (name your concern) means anything. I have given everything about this (name it) all the meaning it has for me, and so on.

I would like you to focus on lesson 5 that tells us *"I am never upset for the reason I think"*, then lesson 6 *"I am upset because I see something that is not there"* and lesson 7 *"I see only the past."*

I am always upset because of something from the past. Allow the Holy Spirit to bring up something from your past that this represents. If nothing comes to mind continue on with the practice of writing the titles and applying them specifically to the issue at hand. At some point there will be a light bulb moment and the real upset will be revealed to you. As we are willing to look at what the ego is really using to rob our joy, we will realize how meaningless and silly it is.

The ego mind tries to use the darkness of avoidance and denial to keep us captive.

Lesson 45
"God is the Mind with which I think."

*As I practiced this lesson today I came to the realization that until our Mind is One with God, we are always thinking **about** something.*

Thus, we are not thinking from the Source of Thought but *about* something in the illusion-- a counterfeit of the Thought of God. We are not coming from origination; we are coming from past and future.

I would recommend that we just sit quietly as the lesson recommends and let the worldly thoughts flow through our mind. Not thinking about them. Just let them come and go.

A quote from Charles Fillmore, the co-founder of Unity Church, which I have always loved, is this: "*You can't stop the birds from flying over your head, but you can stop them from nesting in your hair.*" So it is with worldly thoughts. They will come and go, but we do not have to think about them. We can observe them and then bring ourselves back to the Mind of God.

I do this by mentally calling out, "God, God, and God!" and allowing my mind to return to the quietness and joy of being one with Our Father and My Self.

Lesson 46
"God is the Love in which I forgive."

This quote from the lesson really stood out for me,
FORGIVENESS IS THE GREAT NEED OF THIS WORLD.

Forgiveness as the Course uses it would solve all the problems we could think of in this illusion. In the Course, forgiveness really means *withdrawing judgment* and letting the Holy Spirit's perception be our guide.

This lesson teaches that we must look at any thought in our holy mind that is not loving and forgive it. Even the slightest disturbance about someone or something is an appropriate subject for forgiveness. But most importantly, we must forgive ourselves for all that we are judging about our lives: what we have done, what we have not done and what we have allowed to be done unto us.

Forgive it all with the thought from the title of this lesson. "*GOD is the Love in which I forgive*" (myself). And we know Love never fails. As we forgive ourselves for what we are holding against ourselves, the blocks to Love's Real Presence will be removed and we will again know ourselves as the Holy Child of God that we have always been and always will be.

In this awareness the windows of Heaven will open and Blessings beyond imagination will flow in and through our lives.

Lesson 47
"God is the strength in which I trust."

There is not much I can add to the message of this lesson. It is very clear.

Until we surrender to God the outcome and the working out of all things, we will be in fear. The belief that we can be without God is the reason. It is the most fearful condition of which we can conceive.

We can never be without God because this is how we were created. We were created in the Thought of Oneness and it is in this Oneness we remain, no matter how many crazy imaginings we come up with. We are One with God and God is Strength. Therefore, we can only be Strong in the Lord and in His Power and Might.

When you have time, please read this lesson in its entirety. It is a jewel.

Lesson 48
"There is nothing to fear."

This lesson is probably one of the shortest lessons in the book but one of the powerful.

The only weapon the ego has is our belief that fear is real. It is our fear of fear that is the problem. If we could just be aware that this belief is not a prediction or caution from God, fear would lose its power. Remembering this lesson will bring us back to a state of mind where we remember that fear is not of God, but strength is.

One of my favorite sayings is: *There is nothing to fear-- God is here.* In this awareness, we open our minds to the Love and Strength of God.

By the Grace of God, we return to the Peace that is our Divine Right.

Lesson 49
"God's Voice speaks to me all through the day."

*It is not enough for us to accept the fact that God's Voice speaks to us all through the day. The real purpose of this lesson is to teach us to **listen** to His Voice.*

God is doing His part; we are learning to naturally do our part. I recommend that you sit quietly and just think the word God, God, God (with a smile on your face). You are allowing yourself to come into the Presence of a Being that adores you. Think how you would act in the *outer realm* if you were approaching someone whom you knew loved you beyond measure and was longing to be with you. This *is* the energy in which we should open our minds to hear God's Voice.

In the beginning, you may think you are making up what you hear. Soon you will become comfortable with the only communication that is Real, that being between the Creator and the Creation.

God is here now lovingly speaking to you.... "Listen!"

Lesson 50
"I am sustained by the Love of God."

Oh, how I love this lesson!!! It is one of my favorites.

To me it is a love letter from Jesus. How simple is peace of mind. We must allow ourselves to be loved by Love. To do this, we must vibrate at the energy of Love. This is why the Course mentions forgiveness so often. If we are holding unloving thoughts against our sisters and brothers, we will believe that God is withholding love from us.

A quote from ACIM that will help us to accept this is: *"The way to God is through forgiveness here. There is no other way."* (ACIM)[12]

There is no other way because God is Love and the blocks to Love's presence must be removed from our minds. As we do our inner work and these blocks are seen as nothing, we will trust the Love of God to sustain us in all things. The degree to which you trust God's Love to sustain us is the degree to which we have forgiven the world of illusion.

"Such is the Kingdom of Heaven. Such is the resting place where your Father has placed you forever." (ACIM)[13]

---

[12] W-256.1
[13] W-50

Lesson 51
"The review covers the following: lessons 1 - 5."

The review of Lesson 5 sums up the other four lessons.

The ego is constantly trying to tell us what everything means and what it is telling us is that we are vulnerable and pitiful and must use attack thoughts to be safe. How foolish this system is. We are the visible form of God. What could cause us to feel the need to attack? Only an erroneous identification could cause a Son of God to accept such an insane premise.

We are not alone, we are not vulnerable and we are not the body. We are the Beloved Creation of a Loving Creator and we dare to accept this now and return to the Kingdom from which we have never departed except in a dream.

Wake up Sleeping Beauty.... Wake up.

Lesson 52
"Today's we will review: lessons 6 - 10."

Each of the reviews has a short paragraph about the lesson. If you have time (and/or willingness), please read each one. They are so helpful.

The reviews that we are working with today are telling us that we have made up a frightening world in which we think we live. We believe in a world in which we are victims of a fearful god. We start from this false premise and then proceed to scare ourselves. God is Love and Love only gives Goodness and Mercy and Strength. This is reality. We have been taught the opposite about God. Now is the time to allow our minds to know and to totally accept that we have been wrong and to allow the Course to, once and for all, lead us back to the Memory of our Loving Father.

Love Never Fails us and God is Love. Let's live from this Truth. Let's stop hurting ourselves with the silly illusions of the ego mind. They are not there except in our imagination.

GOD IS LOVE. Let us trust this.

Lesson 53
"Today we will review: lessons 11 - 15."

I chose the review of this lesson because it really speaks to the problems of the world.

The *world* in which we live is the representation of our past thoughts. We are seeing these images reflected outward on a daily basis. The problem is that these thoughts do not materialize immediately so we often forget that these are our own ideas showing up in form. Thus, an insane or non-loving experience happens today and we think about this again, thus, sending out this energy to return tomorrow.

If we could just stop our minds from analyzing and thinking through past events, we would see a different present. Just think of this as we do with mail that we drop off at the post office or in a mailbox. That mail does not arrive until another day. So it is with our thoughts. What we think today may not show up until tomorrow or longer. When they do show up we can be wise enough to know that this is the past showing up and refuse to accept this in our present.

We will begin to learn to judge not according to appearances, but to judge righteously. To *judge righteously* is to allow the Holy Spirit to be the Vision that we use about all that occurs. In this way, we stop the madness and allow the Beauty and Grace of God's world to be all we experience.

Let there be peace on earth and let it begin with me and my thinking.

Lesson 54
"These are the reviews for today: lessons 16 - 20."

Let's realize the awesome power of our thoughts.

Even those thoughts that seem to float through while we are watching a movie or TV have power. *"All thinking produces form at some level."* (ACIM)[14] I like to think of myself as a forgiveness person. I would suggest that we become very, very aware of our thoughts and catch the ones we do not want to have manifest in our world. Give those thoughts to Spirit. We can do so by saying the forgiveness prayer (found at lesson 16 "A Path To Peace") or by simply saying *Spirit, I invite you into this thought.*

It is the ego's ploy: to either have us become unconscious of what we are thinking, or to tell us that these thoughts have no meaning. Well, they do not have meaning in the Kingdom but here in the illusion they make the world we see. Let's make it a practice to watch our thoughts about others and ourselves and return our holy minds to its original state of peace and love and joy. It is all up to us.

We were given free will about what to think. The best use of free will (in the illusion) is to give it back to the Father.

Thy Will be Done in the kingdom of my mind and everything else will be added unto us.

Lesson 55
"Today's review includes: lessons 21 - 25."

This is a wonderful message about surrender.

What I hear is the reminder that when there is something we think we want in this world, it is simply an indication of our erroneous belief that we could be separate from our God and True Selves. When we know who we are, there is nothing else that we could desire. If we mentally followed everything that we desire here, we would come to the core issue. What we desire here is the experience of peace, love and joy. When we come to this realization we will accept what we truly desire.

Our Inheritance from God is all that was given to us in our

---

[14] T-2.VI.9.14

Creation! It is ours already unless we think our good comes from the ego world in which we seem to live. Most of us have had enough experience to know that the ego gives only to take away.

Thus, in any situation the only real desire we can have is the Will of God. Our only prayer must become, *God's Will is done.*

Everyone is happy. Thank you, Mother/Father God.

Lesson 56
"Our review for today includes: lessons 26 - 30."

"Yet perfect security and complete fulfillment are my inheritance."(ACIM)[15]

How wonderful to be reminded of this Truth. This is our inheritance right now. But most of us are not experiencing this. And why not? The ego wants to keep the answer to this question obscure to us because the answer is so simple that we would be insane not to do what it suggests. The answer is that we are constantly attacking others and ourselves with our thoughts. We think that these attack thoughts weaken those we are thinking about, but they only weaken us. We were not meant to attack each other and ourselves. We are out of our element when so doing. We were created from Love to Love. Anything else causes such a strain in our energy field and we feel vulnerable and threatened.

Remember, the Course tells us that we always attack ourselves first. If something happens, we first think an ego thought which tells us that we are somehow out of control. Then, the ego says to regain control of the situation we must equalize the situation by attacking back. This only leads to further feelings of vulnerability that blocks our inheritance from God.

Let us become aware of our thoughts. If something happens that is not to our liking, immediately invite the Holy Spirit into our interpretation of the event. At minimum, we can tell ourselves that we do not know what anything, including this, means.

---

[15] W-56.1(26)5

In this way we leave a space in our mind for the Vision of the Holy Spirit.

Lesson 57
"Our review for today includes: lessons 31 - 35."

To any of us going through an uncomfortable experience right now, this lesson could make us angry. It sounds like we can just wave a magic wand and become free of the circumstances. Well, it is not exactly a magic wand that we wave. But it is a sort of magic.

Change your thinking-- change your life. We have all heard this many times. The thing that we often do not realize is that it is unconscious thoughts that are bringing us the experiences from which we so want to be free. The first step is to consciously accept that the world we see is a reflection of the thoughts we held in mind up to now. This is hard to do at times. We feel as though we have been doing our inner work and using positive affirmations. Do we realize how little time we spend doing this and all the time we spend with the thoughts that make up the unpleasant world we see?

You probably know what I am going to say is the next step. You are right, **say the forgiveness prayer.** (Located at lesson 16) Then, whenever thoughts about the current situation come to mind, remind yourself gently that *that's been forgiven*. Do not entertain any further thoughts or you will bring the same events to yourself in the future.

(The origin of the Forgiveness Prayer occurred because students of the "Course" would often ask, what exactly does the "Course" mean when it talks about forgiveness. As always, I took this to Jesus in meditation and the forgiveness prayer was received.)

Another good thought to use when we begin to ruminate about what is occurring now is to say, "*Holy Spirit I invite you into this thought.*" These are our magic wands that will remove the remnants of past error thoughts and bring us a future filled with joy. Remember, the past is over. It can touch us not. That is, unless we allow ourselves the cheap thrill of thinking about it all over again. The choice is ours, victim or victor. *Chose Victor.*

Lesson 58
"These ideas for today's review: lessons 36 - 40."

When we see this lesson in the context of the lessons preceding it, we can finally realize why this may not be manifesting in our lives at the moment. It is when we know our holiness that we can accept and live the Truth this lesson offers.

Our Father is doing all that is promised. However, if we are not living from a position of knowing how holy we truly are, we are blocking the acceptance of this into our awareness. Truth is so simple. Give up what you do not want. Keep what you do.

We do not want to feel guilty and thus block our Father's gifts. However, we seem to value judgment and attack more. I trust that none of us would be continuing to do this if, when tempted to attack others or ourselves, we would remember the true choices. We were created in the image and likeness of our Creator.

We are holy, very, very holy. We can relax in the knowledge that ALL that the Father has is ours now.

Lesson 59
"The ideas for review today: lessons 41 - 45."

While reading this review, it seemed there was not much to be added to what was already shared.

However, as I meditated, I realized the issue is not whether God goes with us (thus we are safe and provided for) but rather, do we remember this while going about our lives. More importantly, do we believe this? *"If you knew Who walks beside you on the way that you have chosen, fear would be impossible."*(ACIM)[16] The practice is becoming conscious of God's

Presence all the time and everywhere. We would feel at Home everywhere if we kept this Truth in mind. We can do this by repeating the idea frequently to ourselves until it fills all the seemingly empty, lonely, longing places in our mind.

The Bible tells us, Of myself I can do nothing. Our Course tells us, you cannot be of yourself. We are One with God and always will be. Our part is to train our minds to think from this position. We are not trying to make this true. We are reminding ourselves that this is the Truth.

"How can I suffer when love and joy surround me through Him?"(ACIM)17

Lesson 60
"The ideas for today's review: lessons 46 - 50."

We wish to return to our natural state of Peace and Love and Joy.

We cannot wake up from our dream of guilt and separation in a state of fear. In order to return to the Kingdom of Heaven, we must see everyone and everything as an Image of God. How else can we return to our awareness of Oneness with each other and with our Heavenly Father?

One of my favorite lines in the Course comes from this lesson and it has served me well. It is this: *"Everyone and everything I see will lean toward me to bless me. I see in everyone my dearest Friend."* How wonderful life can be when we travel through time with this as our mantra! Fear becomes impossible when we see the Holy Spirit in everyone.

What can frighten us when we are in the presence of Love and Joy?

---

[16] T-18.III.3.2
[17] W-59.1.5

The Lessons Illuminated
Lessons & Review of ACIM 61-90

GOD'S PLAN = FORGIVE = BE HAPPY.
How simple is this plan, and it is the only plan that works.

Illustrated by Cathleen Schott

Lesson 61
"I am the light of the world."

One thing you cannot say about A COURSE IN MIRACLES is that it is dull!

Before we came to the teachings of the Course, we were taught not to think of ourselves as magnificent and wonderful. We were told that this was conceited. We were asked, "Who do you think you are?" Well, I guess we have the answer to this question now. We are the Creation of a Loving Father who can only create like Himself.

If we were One with God, how arrogant it would be for us to think that we are not the Light of the World. While meditating on this thought we can allow God's Vision to be our thoughts. Then, this idea becomes natural and easy for us.

We are the Light of the World because of Who created us. We did not create ourselves, although we did make a sad parody of God's Idea. Now we are letting go of this ego idea of what we are and allow our Love Light to shine into our world. We are here to be bringers of salvation. To do this, we must first accept the message of this lesson for ourselves. We are here to bring the Love Light wherever we go and to whatever is happening.

This is our job and our joy.

Lesson 62
"Forgiveness is my function as the light of the world."

There is no doubt that we all desire happiness.

The reason for the depth of our desire is that happiness is our natural state. We were created to be happy and strong. We do not deserve to suffer. Suffering is a false belief we have accepted from our ego thinking.

There is nothing we can do or ever could do to cause us to deserve to be anything other than what our Creator meant us to be. Nothing outside of us can hurt, injure, or make us sad.

The ego has guided us to think that something is to blame for our ills. When we accept that there is nothing, no one, and not even ourselves to blame for our condition, we would have true forgiveness.

Then, as this lesson instructs us, we will forgive and be happy.

Lesson 63
"The light of the world brings peace to every mind through my forgiveness."

"How holy are you... How blessed are you."

If we would keep reminding ourselves of this, the world would be truly blessed by our presence. It is when we feel guilty and judging that we, and the world, forget that we are all the light of the world.

As our light gets covered over with error thought, we begin to believe we are *not* as God created us. This lesson recommends to frequently remind ourselves of our true Identity. Thus, we can go through our lives as the Love Light we are. Those we meet will be truly blessed. It is so much easier for others to feel the Love Light when they are in the presence of someone who is not judging them.

Let us go out into our world and be the highest example of Love for others to follow. Thus we bring peace to the mind of all we meet.

Lesson 64
"Let me not forget my function."

Let me forgive and be happy.

It is a good idea for us to remind ourselves of this quote, from our lesson, many times during the day. It is so easy to think from the ego standpoint of; let me be RIGHT and be happy. We all know how *well* this has worked for us. It certainly has not led us to the peace of mind that is our Divine Inheritance. We have been given a function here on earth and that is to forgive.

Our Identity is a Being who is One with God. Our awareness of this Oneness is blocked by judgments, blame, and being in the past and future. We cannot experience happiness with these blocks in our mind. Removing these patterns of error thought is what forgiveness is for. We were created to be happy and this lesson is reminding us that this is so.

No matter how *right* we may be, no matter how many people may agree that we are *right*, happiness will elude us. The ego keeps this fact hidden even though we have had this experience over and over and over again.

Remember, forgiveness is simply the withdrawal of judgment. I like to think about the saying we often use in our meetings: *holding a grievance is like drinking poison and expecting the other person to die*. Looking at un-forgiveness in this way makes it a lot easier to let go of our ego judgments.

FORGIVE AND BE HAPPY!!! Simple, simple, simple.

Lesson 65
"My only function is the one God gave me."

Why would we want another function?

The previous lesson taught us to forgive is to be happy. It can only be that we really do not know what happiness is. Happiness comes only from fulfilling the Will of God. It is God's Will that we receive Love from God and extend it to others.

When we do other than this, we are out of alignment with God and Ourselves. Once out of alignment all sorts of ego things begin to come our way. In this state of unconsciousness we accept the ego lies to be what is true about us, such as, sickness, suffering, and death.

All of this is the price of being *right* and withholding forgiveness. In the event that you are having a problem letting go of an ego thought, just tell yourself to be a little willing to be willing to forgive it.

Holy Spirit will use the slightest of willingness to come in and do it for us.

Lesson 66
"My happiness and my function are one."

Suggestion: Read this lesson in its entirety. It is a very important step toward God's Will for happiness for us.

Don't you love the logic of our Course? We are not asked to accept its teachings on blind faith, or on the premise that someday, in the by and by, we will understand its message. No, our Course is logical, loving and practical. Forgive and you will align yourself with the Will of your Creator. The Will of our Creator is perfect happiness for us now.

We can be out of alignment with our Father's will when we will something different for others or ourselves, in the way of judgment. Many times we judge another in order to balance the guilt that we feel about ourselves, and our thoughts and actions.

This is the ego's way to happiness. It is not our way. Our way is the way of our Father, and that is only the way of forgiveness.

Forgiveness = happiness. Let this be the thought that will lead us to awaken to our True Identity.

Lesson 67
"Love created me like itself."

"LOVE CREATED ME LIKE ITSELF."

God is Love, so Love created me like Itself. Let's review some of the attributes of God given to us in the Course. God is love, peace, joy, abundance, wholeness, freedom, and beauty. Therefore, if Love/God created us like Itself, we can only be an expression of these traits.

How can we be sick when Wholeness created us like Itself? How can fear seem so real to us when Love created us like Itself? We are either as God created us, or we are not. As it says in the Bible, *I have set before thee life and death.... Choose life.* Let's choose life by keeping our minds focused on the attributes of God, and not let the ego fool us into thinking we are what the illusion says we are.

We are the visibility and tangibility of God. This is the Truth for us and this is what sets us free.

Lesson 68
"Love holds no grievances."

The lessons are so beautiful, powerful and healing

When I was meditating with the message in this lesson, it became very clear to me why we could possibly fear God. As we discussed previously, God is Love, and to fear Love is insane. Through the ego guidance we have redefined what love is and then projected this onto our Creator.

In the ego realm, love can give and love can take away. Love can approve and disapprove. Love can be kind or withholding. All these attributes we can have and still feel that we love each other. When we project this way of loving onto God, there is little wonder that we are fearful of Him. We find it hard to surrender to, *Thy Will be done.*

We are unconsciously aware of our little and not so little *sins*. We think that surely God is holding these against us, as we do with others. From this moment on, let's give up the idea that Love can hold a grievance and punish for it. Love (God) holds no grievances, NONE. That which you are holding against yourself or another has no meaning in the Kingdom of God.

LOVE/GOD HOLDS NO GRIEVANCES!!!

This is the truth. We are innocent and loved as we were created. Therefore, let us take our rightful place in the Kingdom and allow Love's Will to be done on earth as it is in Heaven.

Lesson 69
"My grievances hide the light of the world in me."

What a picturesque way Jesus has of describing what grievances do to our holy minds.

I am sure we have all noticed that when we are judging and blaming and holding grievances against our brother/sisters, how very difficult it is to see clearly. At this point in our awakening we know that there is another way of looking at the situation. Somehow, the clouds or fog (fear of God) seem to block our clarity. This is why it is so important, to have Someone to turn to for help to make our way through the clouds of guilt without fear.

We ask our Dear Friend, the Holy Spirit, to guide us back to our peace. When our asking is genuine, it is amazing how quickly we make our way through the clouds and return to the Love Light that is our true Identity.

How wonderful it is to know that our grievances are really nothing. They can be let go and easily brushed aside with our willingness to be led back to our True Selves.

Lesson 70
"My salvation comes from me."

How I love the line above. I have used it so very often in my life. It is very comforting to think of our big brother, Jesus, right there with us to comfort and guide.

It may help to make this lesson a little more practical, if we realize that the Course uses the words salvation and happiness as the same thing. With this in mind, it becomes easier to practice the ideas put forth in this lesson. Nothing can help or heal us except forgiveness. This is our function here. This is our gift. It is only guilt that teaches us that someone or something outside of our mind can cause us to lose the peace and joy of God. When feeling guilty, we do not want to remember that God is the First Cause of all. We are too afraid to believe this, so we project our hurts, pains, and even deaths on to something in the illusion. If this or that were only different, we could be saved/happy.

If we really thought it was our own guilt making us unhappy, we would have to look inside our minds for the cure. The ego says; do not look within, or you will recoil as if from a poisonous snake. What a tremendous lie we have accepted! If we were to look within, as the Course says, *we would weep at our own magnificence.* We would also realize that God is the Giver of all good, nothing else.

The guilt that we are feeling must be, simply, error thought, and the result of ego guidance. It is not real. It is like a cloud. There is nothing we can do that can change our Father's Love for us. He wants us to be happy and we want to be happy. This is our natural state. God's Will for us is perfect happiness, NOW.

No matter what we have done; no matter what we have not done, we are still His Beloved in Whom He is well-pleased.

Lesson 71
"Only God's plan for salvation will work."

How simple is happiness...do what works and do not do what has never worked.

The ego dictates that our happiness is circumstance-dependent. This has never brought us lasting happiness. Oh, in the beginning, it seems to bring us some measure of relief and seeming happiness, but with this too, the ego robs from us.

If the changes we make under the direction of the ego are valuable to us, the ego will tell us to be careful or we will lose them. If the changes do not bring us the desired result, the ego will point out how wrong we were to have made this move, and the discomfort will never end. One cannot win with the ego. It is a thief. Let us remember that the ego can only suggest thoughts to us. We do not have to accept them, just as the Holy Spirit's guidance can only be received by our own willingness to hear it.

As we go about our day, let us do so with the Holy Spirit's Voice in our mind. Ask the Holy Spirit the questions suggested in the lesson and be willing to accept the Holy Spirit's help in following the answers. The Voice of the Holy Spirit is the Voice of our Real Self. *"My peace I give unto you. Peace comes from God through me to you."* (ACIM)[18] We are simply asking for what is ours already. This is the Peace that comes from knowing that we have the never failing Wisdom, of the Father, to be our guide.

What more can we possibly ask?

Lesson 72
"Holding grievances is an attack on God's plan for salvation."

In this lesson, we are looking at the ego's plan for salvation/happiness with the intent to learn to disregard it.

I think it is important to first note that we are not the ego. We are the Creation of our Heavenly Father. So the plan from the ego to attack God's plan is not OUR plan.

It is the ego suggestion coming from an original tiny mad idea at which we remembered not to laugh. The mad idea was that we could be separate from each other, our Creator and Ourselves. From this mad idea came all the seeming problems of the world. The issue is not that we had the original mad idea, but that these problems and trials are the result of our *continuing* to accept this mad idea.

---

[18] T-10.III.6.6

Even in this insane state of mind, we are not alone. God has not abandoned us. Somewhere in our mind, we remember our Identity and yearn to experience only this. We have only to turn back to the Altar of God and ask for help.

"What is salvation, (happiness) Father? I do not know. Tell me, that I may understand."(ACIM)[19] *"He will answer. Be determined to hear."*(ACIM)[20]

Lesson 73
"I will there be light."

Again, I recommend you read this lesson in the Workbook.

The important message of this lesson is that God's Will and our will are the same. There is no doubt we want to be happy and healthy. However, the problem arises because what we have taught ourselves will not bring this about. With the ego leading, we have raised control to a very high level. The thought of trusting God's Will to provide and protect us has become obscure.

The ego tells us that to rid ourselves of the blocks to our happiness and health, we must project our judgments and grievances outside our minds and into the minds of our brothers and sisters. We *righteously* judge and exclude parts of the Sonship in an attempt to align ourselves, again, with what we subconsciously know will bring our good to us.

We know that to align ourselves with God's Will is the way to peace. However, the ego tells us how guilty and dark we are, and that before we can accept our Oneness with God, we must rid ourselves of our *sins*. It tells us that in order to do this we must project these sins onto others. Thus judgment and grievances seem to be the way to happiness. Of course, this leads us in the wrong direction.

---

[19] W-72.12.2-4
[20] W-72.12.5&6

We know the way out of hell is within. Let us begin today. Surrender to God's plan for our happiness, which is forgiveness, not projection. Whenever the temptation to blame and judge comes to mind, remind yourself,

"I will there be light. Darkness is not my will." (ACIM)[21]

Lesson 74
"There is no will but God's."

Let's review for a moment.

God's Will for us is perfect happiness NOW! We are told this time after time in our Course. Somehow, when we are out of peace and joy, we think we have to convince our Heavenly Father to help us to return to our natural state.

We falsely feel that we are not worthy. Therefore, God needs to be begged or manipulated, by metaphysical methods, to bestow on us what is our Divine Right. We are not in conflict with God in our desire to experience peace, love, joy, abundance, wholeness, beauty and freedom. This is God's Idea for us.

Somehow, the ego has convinced us, God is withholding our gifts because of the guilt we may be experiencing. But, there is nothing we can do to change Eternal Love for us.

Let's be willing to recall this truth the next time we find ourselves experiencing something besides God's Will. Remind yourself gently and often, *I am not in conflict with God in my willingness to experience peace, love and joy.* The only problem I have is to let go of ego thinking through forgiveness. We now allow ourselves to know the Magnificent Creations of a Loving Creator that we are.

Then, all Good will return to our awareness with no effort at all.

---

[21] W-73.II.5&6

Lesson 75
"The light has come."

This lesson brings to my mind a story I heard some time ago.

It was about a man who had been blind since birth. Eventually a procedure was developed so that his sight was restored. When he first looked out through his sighted eyes, he was very frightened. It seems, that although he could physically see, his brain could not compute what he was taking in.

I think it is somewhat like this, with us, when we allow the *lens* of the ego to be removed from our eyes. We begin to see clearly through the vision of the Holy Spirit. We really do not know how to compute what we are seeing. This is why the lesson *"I do not understand anything I see"* (ACIM)[22] is so appropriate.

We do not know what anything means, but the Holy Spirit does know. The Holy Spirit brings to us the spiritual light in which we view the world. What was fearful or questionable becomes the visibility of God, or something to heal our mind.

How safe we feel knowing that we do not have to take care of ourselves. To know that we are in the *Hands* of our Real Self is so, so comforting. We can rest in God. We are almost Home.

I wonder if you will join me in feeling how happy Jesus sounds in this lesson! I am willing to match His energy. I love Him so much. He is our wonderful older brother.

Lesson 76
"I am under no laws but God's."

As we think of the laws and rules which we have set up for ourselves, we must see that although they were set up to make us feel safe, they have done the opposite. Any law/rule ritual etc. in which we believe, can be easily disproved by something in the

---

[22] W-51.3. (3)1

illusion.

The *laws* of health show this to us very clearly. Smoking will give you lung cancer. How many people do we know about who never smoked and still endured the belief they had lung cancer? Exercise keeps you healthy. The same irony can often be seen here. Eating certain foods will give you ill health, thus, teaching us the fear of food. You get the picture.

The Course tells us that there is no immunity in the form. There is nothing here that can help or hurt us unless we believe it can. There is no law in form that does not have an exception. But, God's Laws are certain and never fail. His Law is the Law of Love. Love gives only good. It never takes, no matter what. We are loved by our Creator. We were created perfect and it is thus we remain. We were created in joy and peace. This is all God sees. It is good, very, very good. We must learn to see this way, if we are to be in alignment with our Creator.

Nothing we do, or do not do, can change Eternal Love for us. Nothing we do, or do not do, can change God's Will for us to be happy and joyful. And we thank you God that this is so.

We allow this to be the only Truth in our minds.

Lesson 77
"I am entitled to miracles."

Let's really contemplate what this lesson is teaching us. You are the physical expression of an Invisible God. It would be good to say, "I (your name) am entitled to miracles. I am entitled right now in the present moment." This is not a request we are making or a wish expressed, this is our Divine Right to miracles that we are talking about.

We remember that a miracle is a shift in perception from fear to love. I am entitled to a perception that is only loving because of what I truly am. We are Creations of Love, forever One with our Creator. How could we possibly change this? We can't. But we can think that we have changed this when we do not see our brothers/sisters as Creations of Love. We can easily be fooled by their own mistaken identity, which causes them to act from fear. How fearful it is to not remember that we are all one.

However, when we turn our perceptions over to the Holy Spirit, everyone wins and no one loses. We reclaim what we were entitled to all along, which is the miracle of remembering that we remain as God created us. Thus God's Will is done on earth as it is in heaven.

Lesson 78
"Let miracles replace all grievances."

As I mentioned before, please read the lessons in their entirety.

I think that this lesson can be summarized in the line that says *"Someone, perhaps, you fear and even hate; someone you think you love who angered you; someone you call a friend, but whom you see as difficult at times or hard to please, demanding, irritating or untrue to the ideal he should accept as his, according to the role you set for him."* "ACCORDING TO THE ROLE YOU SET FOR HIM."

This is where our grievances come from. We have expectations of each other and when these are not met, we judge and blame others for the fact that we have lost our peace. How the ego loves to keep the conflict and the drama alive. The ego can only keep it alive by causing us to be unconscious and react from the world's way of being, instead of seeing it through the Holy Spirit's (our Real Self) eyes.

The Holy Spirit would remind us that we are never upset for the reason we think. We are always upset due to something from our past. From this vantage point, we can correct error thoughts from our past and allow the miracle to awaken us to Who we truly are.

Lesson 79
"Let me recognize the problem so it can be solved."

Again, we see how simple salvation (happiness) is.

If we are asking for a problem to be solved, and that is not the problem, then no matter how often the seeming problem seems to be resolved in the outer world, it does not solve the problem. We can change homes, jobs, or mates, thinking this will bring us lasting peace of mind, only to have another issue turn up in our lives. Many times we have *fixed* the outer world, only to come to a place where we think that there is always something else. We have learned to accept that if we are in the body there will always be problems. However, it is only through a path like the Course or other high teachings that we learn that this was not our problem all along. Our only problem was and is that we believe that we can be separate from Our True Self and God. How ridiculous.

There is only God. God came first and filled all there is. Let's begin today to practice thinking that there is nothing in the outer world that will satisfy our longings. We are longing for the Love of God and we have this and are this already.

Let's ask the first question of the Holy Spirit. How can I experience God's Love? I like to say, "Father reveal Yourself to me in this." Then wait and listen. You will be told.

Lesson 80
"Let me recognize my problems have been solved."

Today, let us give ourselves the gift of a moment of silence.

Whenever a problem seems to present itself to our mind, whatever the issue may be, the solution is the awareness of the Peace of God. *"I am with you always, even unto the end of the world."* (ACIM)[23] There is not a moment that we are not One with the Peace, Joy and Love of our Creator. God never leaves us. We must not leave God by thinking thoughts that the ego suggests to us.

This lesson asks us to do our part when seeming difficulties

---

[23] T-8.IV.2.4

arise. When we take a moment and allow the Peace of God to fill our consciousness, all problems disappear. The Peace of God is everything we ever wanted, and this is available to us at our request. It may take practice for us to release the idea that a problem requires our *great* thinking process. As we become more and more willing to accept the only solution, we will find it more natural than breathing.

God is our heart's only desire. That's all, one problem, one solution. Amen

Lesson 81
"Our ideas for review today are: lessons 61 & 62."

During this time of the year when the world celebrates the Resurrected Christ, it is good that our lesson today reminds us that we are the light of the world. This is not something that we have control over. We are the light of the world whether we choose this for ourselves or not. The only thing we have control over is our acceptance of this.

Let me today crucify any self-identification that tells us we are not the Son of God. This is done through forgiveness, which is the letting go of any thought that is not the Thought of God.

Let us allow this day to be another major step toward our Great Awakening. We are as God created us, and nothing else matters.

Lesson 82
"We will review these ideas today: lessons 63 & 64."

I trust that we will never fail to realize how important forgiveness is to our Awakening.

The Course actually tells us that *"The way to God is through forgiveness here. THERE IS NO OTHER WAY."*(ACIM)[24] I believe

---

[24] W-256.1.1&2

this is one of the most important statements in the Course.

As we talked about earlier in these writings, our heart's desire is to remember that we are One with God. We have been given a simple and direct path to this experience. Why would we allow some crazy perception to keep us from this?

This lesson expresses there are many things that threaten the ego, because the ego is such a vulnerable part of our mind. Our choice is to feel hurt or betrayed or rejected, etc.; or to remember we are one with the strength of God. Surely when we see it in this light, the choice is clear.

"What could you choose between but life or death." (25)
Choose life, Choose Love! Choose Joy!

Lesson 83
"Today let us review these ideas: lessons 65 & 66."

We are reminded that the only function we have is to be happy, and to be happy we must think the Thoughts of God. That is why forgiveness and happiness are one. God created us in His Joy. Our mind is always joyful. However, we often cover this up with thoughts that do not match the energy of God and our True Selves.

We have made so many false idols that we thought would bring us happiness, only to have them fail relentlessly. Nothing can BRING us happiness. We ARE happiness already. Our job and our joy is to extend the peace and love in which we were created, and to be vigilant that we do not accept the ego's suggestions of what joy is.

Our only function is to be aware of when we are not thinking thoughts in alignment with our Creator, and to let these thoughts go into the nothingness from which they came.

Lesson 84
"Ideas for today's review: lessons 67 & 68."

How important it is to think with the Mind of God!

To allow our Minds to wander into *ego-land* is more than just to have the experience of the cheap thrill, which we have come to expect from this. It is actually attacking our Identity. Jesus is saying we are ATTACKING our true Self, not just ignoring or forgetting Who we are.

Is it little wonder that when we withhold love by holding a grievance against someone or something, we feel so fearful and vulnerable? Only the awareness of our True Identity as Lovers brings us the peace we truly desire.

The ego tells us that holding a grievance against someone will bring us the *peace* of being right. However, we have all lived long enough, and have used this ego technique enough to know that this *peace* is instant but not lasting.

Let us remember that whenever we are out of peace, it is because we have the thought, *"Now I can't love you"*. In this thought, the attack on Our Self is experienced. We are Lovers, not blamers, nor judges, nor attackers. *We are the Love of God in expression. How blessed we are!!!*

Lesson 85
"Review will cover these ideas: lessons 69 & 70."

How often our dear elder brother, Jesus, reminds us that we were created in Joy and in Joy we remain.

The ego would have us think that this or that must happen in order for us to be happy. When we finally realize that the Divine Order is; God through me and out into the world, then we will never be a victim of the world again.

God is our Source. We have not left our Source. We cannot leave our Source. There is nowhere else to go except to our insane ego point of view. To hold a grievance against the world by thinking that an outer event has robbed us of our joy, peace and love is absurd. Our good does not come to us; it comes through us. If this were held in our mind, there would never ever be an occasion to judge or blame another for our state of mind.

We are the Beloved Child of a Loving God. We can rest.

Lesson 86
"Today we will review: lessons 71 & 72."

God's Plan = forgive = be happy.
How simple is this plan, and this is the ONLY plan that will work.

We all know that happiness is not available to us as we carry slights, hurts, and incriminations in our holy minds. This is not the natural state of the mind of a Son of God. When out of our natural state we feel strained, and strain leads us to fear, and fear leads to projection. Thus, we have the condition of the world we see all around us.

The ego constantly reminds us of what has happened that seems to have hurt us. It tells us that if we were to release these thoughts we would be open to the possibility of these events happening once more. We know that the opposite is the truth. What we think about increases. Thoughts HELD in mind produce after their kind. I know we all are aware of this, but it is always helpful to be reminded. *Let's accept God's plan and be happy.*

Lesson 87
"Today we will review: lessons 73 & 74."

How wonderful it is to be reminded of the Truth.

There is no will but God's Will. True, God gave us free will in our Creation, but as we have experienced, the only appropriate use of free will is to give it back to God. God's Will be done on earth as it is in Heaven should be our prayer. How wonderful to know that God's Will is Heaven on Earth.

We have tried to make another will but it has only led to chaos and disaster. All the control, that the ego guides us to make use of, ultimately has to be released if we want to return to our peace.

As we surrender to the Will of God, our experience becomes one of goodness and safety. Trust is the first characteristic of a Teacher of God. What we are giving our trust to, is the Will of God. And, as the Course teaches---*Trust will solve all problems now.*

Lesson 88
"Today we will review: lessons 75 & 76."

The Light of the Truth about ourselves is now available to us.

We remain as God created us. There is nowhere else for us to place our faith. God is the author of our lives. We gladly surrender to this. Why wouldn't we? He has placed before us all the gifts of the Spirit and of the Kingdom; is there any reason to choose otherwise?

We have made up little rules of behavior and thought which block the awareness of Who and What we truly are. Surely, as our Course tells us, we are not victims of these laws. However, most of us, for much of our lives, live and die by them. How sad, when we are only accountable to the laws of God. His are the laws of love. Allow the Love to flow through you to your brothers and sisters and be happy. This is God's only law. Love God, love yourself and love your neighbor.

To do this is to have the Kingdom restored to our awareness.

Lesson 89
"These are our review for today: lessons 77 & 78."

The reviews of these lessons contain an important message.

They remind us that we have a function to fulfill given us by God. To fulfill this function, we must accept the gifts of God.

God has given us all we need to fulfill our purpose here. This help remains obscure to us as long as we are using our holy minds to hold grievances against our brothers and sisters in Christ.

We are here to heal our minds. That is all the world is for. As we do our forgiveness work, our mind clears of all the error thoughts we have accumulated, and the Light of God shines through us to all whom we meet. Thus, we become the ministers of God as we were called upon to be.

Send them to us, our Father. We are willing to fulfill your purpose.

Lesson 90
"Today we will review: lessons 79 & 80."

The review of these lessons is helping us withdraw our belief in time.

The Course tells us that the belief in time is one of the defenses we have made against the Truth. The ego would like us to believe that things take time, even spiritual healing. Our dear brother Jesus, is reminding us that all time is now, and that the perceived problems or illnesses and their solution is simultaneous. We do not have to wait *for a time* for healing and solution of problems.

Let us now accept the peace that this awareness brings. "*The problem must be gone because God's answer cannot fail.*" [26] It is only the error thought that we can possibly be separate from the Love of God, which brings us a different experience. We are One with a Timeless, Eternal and Loving Creator. There is nothing that can change this. We can go about our lives unaware of this, but in any *Now Moment*, we can become aware of our Identity, and be healed of anything unlike our Father. Time is not a part of the Kingdom of God. Our only problem has been solved.

Let us now accept the peace that this brings to us.

The Lessons Illuminated
Lessons & Review of ACIM 91-120

WHAT GOOD NEWS TO LEARN,
we were mistaken when we believed that we were sinners and worthy of guilt and pain.

Illustrated by Cathleen Schott

Lesson 91
"Miracles are seen in light."

It is only in the light of Truth that we will realize our magnificence.

In this realization, the need to judge and be fearful will disappear. It is only the darkness of *ego thinking* that obscures our Identity and guides us to find a false identity in the judgments we hold of others. In this darkness we feel alone and vulnerable. However, the darkness is but an illusion. When we see with the Light of the Holy Spirit's Vision, we realize there is indeed nothing to fear.

When I am feeling out of peace, I allow myself to be aware of the thought that is causing it, the darkness, and I pray thus: *Holy Spirit, I invite you into this thought.*

While praying, I visualize a darkened room and think of myself switching on the light. The darkness has no power over the light. In this light we see the miracle that shows us the strength and power that is our Divine Right. Then, we know we are not weak, but strong.

We are strong, not by our own power, but by the Omnipotence of our Heavenly Father, which is ours as well.

Lesson 92
"Miracles are seen in light, and light and strength are one."

Again, I must mention that I only take a few thoughts from the lessons. Please try to go over the lessons in their entirety to receive the full message from Jesus

It is so beautiful and powerful; Miracles are seen in the light. This makes so much sense. The only way we can see clearly is when our mind is free of grievances. When we have removed the blocks to Love's presence, the Light of God is manifest in our lives. In this energy we know for certain that nothing outside us can hurt or injure us. We know that we are as God created us, whole and complete and full of joy.

However, when we are under the ego's guidance, the world seems to be a dark and scary place. We know that the ego's range goes from *suspicious to vicious*. Surely, we cannot know our true Self if we are seeing our brothers and sisters from this viewpoint. When we are in the *suspicious to vicious* energy, we think of ourselves as weak, and then defense and projection become the ego's way to safety.

We know by now that this plan never has given us the strength and peace we deserve. Let us now release the need to see the world through the darkness of the ego and allow the Light of God to shine on us and all we meet.

In this energy, we will experience the constant strength and power that is our Father's Will for us.

Lesson 93
"Light and joy and peace abide in me."

It will serve us well if we were to practice the message in this lesson as often as possible today.

Let's try to decide what will be the trigger for us to practice this message today. I am willing to remind myself of this each time I look at my watch or each time I take a sip of water, etc. I find it so helpful to put our spiritual practices alongside something we do in the outer.

Imagine the joy that is available to us when we totally forgive ourselves for the false concepts we have adhered to about others and ourselves! The Voice for God is constantly telling us of our Father's Will for us. But we have used ego beliefs and concepts to interfere with this message.

We are wrong about who we are. Let us be joyful that this is so. Our sinlessness is GUARANTEED BY GOD. What better guarantee could we have?

When any thought of guilt or fear comes to mind, let us remember we are sinless and light, joy and peace abide in us. We can be so arrogant to disagree with God about this! God created us, and God knows us as we are. This is how it is, whether we accept it or not. Let us accept it. What wonderful news this is. Let it become the Truth of our Being.

"Light and joy and peace abide in me. My sinlessness is guaranteed by God."

Lesson 94
"I am as God created me."

Years ago, I meditated with the message of this lesson and was surprised at the resistance I still had to the use of the word "Son".

I wonder how many women are still struggling with the use of this word as in; "I am His *Son* eternally." At that time, when very new to the Course, I asked Jesus why He used the words *Son* and *Father* and the answer was that the Course is meant to be a comfortable transition for people familiar with the Bible. Using words from the Bible made it easier for these people to relate to its message. Thus, I released the need to be disturbed by a word. A word is simply a symbol twice removed from reality.

Let us get to the *core* of this lesson. "I am as God created me," and God created me in Its image and Likeness. There can be nothing about me that is unlike my Creator. I am whole and complete and filled with joy *eternally*. For some of us there may be blocks to experiencing ourselves in this way. These blocks are a call for us to forgive and release error thought about others and ourselves.

We may still hold concepts that are unlike our Creator. How we fight to keep them! How foolish we have been!

Begin today with this lesson to allow our minds to accept the Truth. We are as GOD created us, not what we have made of ourselves. We are strong, not weak; we are peaceful, not in fear; we are loved and loving, not judgmental. As we keep reminding ourselves about the truth of what we are, accepting this will become as natural as false ego concepts seem to be right now. Whenever the ego tempts us to think something illusionary about ourselves, let us use it as a signal to repeat the title of this lesson in reference to others and ourselves. We let there be Truth and let it begin with our thinking.

"Here is sanity restored."

Lesson 95
"I am one Self, united with my Creator."

I highly recommend that you offer the thought above to all whom you meet today.

I can tell you from experience that you will have a day beyond compare if you do. When I have done this in the past, my energy became so filled with the Love of God that joy was the only emotion I felt. We are One Self. All of us are One, One, One. When we truly realize that we are all the One Idea of God, we find our lives reflecting the Will of God, which is peace, love, joy, abundance, wholeness, beauty, and freedom. What more can one ask in exchange for the little offering we make of releasing the ego suggestions of what we are.

The ego tells us that we are sinful, miserable and beset with pain. This comes from the concept that we can be separate from God and each other. As we remind ourselves of the truth about ourselves, the world is healed with us. Oneness includes all. We are all one Self, united with our Creator.

We are the Beloved of God, now and forever more.

Lesson 96
"Salvation comes from my one Self."

There is little doubt that most of us can relate to the struggle we experience between what the ego says we are and what the Holy Spirit knows we are.

Our Course tells us that the ego will speak first as the interpreter of everything. This voice will tell us that we are sinful, vulnerable, guilty and fearful. Before we became aware that there was another Voice and learned to make this choice, we allowed our mind to think that ego thoughts about ourselves were accurate. This was the self we thought we were. But NOW, oh sweet NOW, we know that there is another choice and this is the choice we make.

Only the Holy Spirit kept our true Identity in trust all the while we were lost in ego-land. Only the Holy Spirit knows our one true Self. *"If we stumble, You will raise us up. If we forget the way, we count upon Your sure remembering. We **wander off**, but You will not forget to call us back."* (ACIM)[25]

Our Course tells us that if we allow our mind to become frantic and confused about who we are, simply get quiet and remind our mind that peace comes from our one Self. The Holy Spirit supports us in this and as we feel this peace, the ego's voice is quiet and we accept the gift of knowing once again that we are One Self united with our Creator.

Lesson 97
"I am spirit."

Who do you say you are?? Are you Spirit or are you the body identification that you were taught to be you? These are the questions to be asked many times until the answer is obvious.

We see the variety of languages, expressions, customs, etc., that this illusion holds. A baby must be taught what is appropriate for his or her family. Once we learn this, these ways seem to be who we are. Of course, they are familiar, but it is time to become familiar with who we truly are.

As we repeat the title of today's lesson, the truth will begin to dawn on us about our true Identity. With this awareness comes all the power and glory of the Universe. Why would we not want

---

[25] W-Review V Introduction 3.2-4

to devote the time and energy to reclaiming our Birthright and all the blessings it brings with it!! *I am Spirit.* This is a simple statement that holds the answer to all problems, illness, and confusion.

This lesson tells us that the gift of surrender to the Truth of Who we are, *"will be multiplied a thousandfold and tens of thousands more. And when it is returned to you, it will surpass in might the little gift you gave as much as does the radiance of the sun outshine the tiny gleam a firefly makes an uncertain moment and goes out."* (ACIM)[26] Surly, there is nothing more important today than to practice this.

I am Spirit, I am Spirit and I am thankful and happy this is so.

Lesson 98
"I will accept my part in God's plan for salvation."

I am sure we have all experienced the wonderful feeling of knowing that we are fulfilling God's Will as we go through an event in our lives.

There is a feeling of certainty and contentment, no matter what it is we are guided to do. Many of us have been called to care for an elderly relative or a sick child and have felt the loving arms of God embracing and supporting our efforts. We do not understand how easily and with little effort that these tasks can be done. So it is when we live our lives in alignment with the Will of God. We have the support of Heaven with us and we feel it.

We know when we are in our right jobs, homes, relationships; and we know when we are not. These are the times when everything may look good from the outside and yet we feel miserable. This is when we are asked to look at our lives and see where we are out of alignment with our soul. When out of alignment, there will be a sense of struggle and strain. We rationalize and justify, proving to ourselves that this is where we are meant to be, doing what we are doing.

---

[26] W-97.6.1&2

If this is the case with you, in some area of your life, first forgive yourself for disregarding the guidance of the Holy Spirit for so long and then surrender, as much as you can, to God's Will. Sometimes we can be only be a little willing to make the called-for change. This is enough to allow the Holy Spirit to work in our lives.

It may be that we are in the right situation, but our thinking is coming from ego. The needed change may be in our perception of the situation. The test for this is to see if what we think and what we say and what we do is congruent. If not, reach down into the Silence and ask yourself which part is from the Holy One Who know God's Will for you. Then ask for help to align with this.

Remember, God's Will is that we are happy and peaceful as we were created.

Lesson 99
"Salvation is my only function here."

To me, a very important line in this lesson is probably the shortest.

It is *"Your Father loves you."* If we would live from this idea, pain in any form would be nonexistent. Our only issue is that we think we can be separate from the Love of God. This is the tiny mad idea at which we forgot to laugh. As we live through the many experiences of this lifetime, just keep in mind that Father has not withdrawn Its Love from us, then we would suffer no more.

This is the lie the ego whispers to us in all our trials: *See, God doesn't love you anymore.* It does not say this blatantly because we would not believe it. But, it whispers it in so many ways. Why did this happen to me? How could this have happened? Why me? All the questions that we ruminate about are really saying that God has withdrawn Its Love. That is the answer the ego gives us silently and cruelly. Today let us forgive ourselves for our mistaken thoughts of our Creator. All the world of sin and pain is not His Will. When any thoughts come to us that seem to disclaim our Father's Love, let us use the statement: *Holy Spirit I invite you into this thought.* Do this as often as necessary until the Love Light shines away our foolish but very painful perceptions. YOUR FATHER LOVES YOU!! We forgive ourselves for thinking otherwise.

To anything that is not joyful, let's remind ourselves, *"Salvation is my only function here. God still is Love, and this is not His Will."* (ACIM)[27] *Thus do you lay forgiveness on your mind and let all fear be gently laid aside, that love may find its rightful place in you and show you that you are the Son of God."* (ACIM)[28]

Lesson 100
"My part is essential to God's plan for salvation."

What this lesson is telling us is that our joy is essential to God's plan for salvation.

We are here to show the world that God's Will is not the disasters that take place, nor the untimely deaths of our loved ones, nor the other sad events which we have ascribed to our Creator. These are not the so-called *acts of God* that have been taught to us. Would a loving earthly parent will such things for his/her child? There is no purpose in this. *"There is no need to learn through pain. And gentle lessons are acquired joyously, and are remembered gladly."* (ACIM)[29]

If we are to help the world and ourselves remember God, we must project a true picture of Him and What He truly is. God is Love and Love only gives and does not take away. If we are to be the ministers of God and play our part in the Great Awakening, we are called to heal our minds of all the error thoughts that block our own awareness of God's Will. His Will for His Creation is to be happy and peaceful. If we are not experiencing this now, we are taught to go to the Holy Spirit and ask for help in removing whatever may be blocking our peace

---

[27] W-99.6.8
[28] W-99.12.5
[29] T-21.I.3.1&2

and joy.

How wonderful that our Heavenly Father is asking us to be happy. Most of us have been taught that sacrifice and martyrdom are the ways to Heaven. But our Course asks us to be happy and gives us the means to be so. *We are indeed blessed to have found this path.*

Lesson 101
"God's Will for me is perfect happiness."

So it is that our dear brother, Jesus, is absolving us from the false idea that we can do something to offend our Eternal God.

There is no sin. We have not changed God's view of us in any way by any of our actions. There is no sin. Nothing we have done or have not done has affected our Birthright in any way. There is nothing in the illusion that can block out the Love of God for us. We are free. Today let us release ourselves from the judgments we may still hold against ourselves. They are nothing. God's Will for us is happiness. Suffering is unnecessary and has no value.

There is nothing we can do to change Eternal Love for us, Nothing. Nothing. Let the past go and know that we are free and pure from Holy Instant to Holy Instant. We are as God created us and nothing can change this.

Take a moment now and look inside and see if there is something you wish you had done or wish that you had not done and release it now into the Light of God's Love. Just as darkness must disappear when a light is turned, on so our *sins* shall vanish when the light of Truth shines on them.

Everything happened as it was written in our contract when we took the form of a body. We let the past go, *now*, into the nothingness from which it came. The past is over. It can touch me not, and we are happy and grateful that this is so.

We accept God's Will for happiness for us now and forever.

Lesson 102
"I share God's Will for happiness for me."

The beauty of this lesson is its simplicity.

We do not want to suffer. How easily we can accept this truth. However, the ego has confused our mind as to what is suffering and what is happiness. We have been guided by the ego to think that keeping past hurts and errors alive in our mind somehow will bring us the happiness to which we are entitled. How faulty is this thinking???

Our happiness comes from letting go into the Present, moment by moment. As we do this we are trusting in the Divine Goodness of the energy of our Creator. There is no value in suffering. It gives us nothing that is useful to our present or future happiness.

Present trust = future joy. How wonderful to know that the Father (Joy) and I are One. This is God's Creation, not ours. God has decreed that we be happy and has given us the only way to be so. That way is to surrender to His Will. Practice this thought in all circumstances in our lives: *I have no power in this, God does.* It is a prayer of complete dependence on God and this is where we will find the happiness and peace which God Wills for us.

"Be happy, for your only function here is happiness."(ACIM)[30]

Lesson 103
"God, being Love, is also happiness."

When love is spoken about as it is in this lesson, it would seem to be insane to be afraid of love.

Because of the way the world portrays love, it is easy to understand why one would be afraid of it. What is called love

---

[30] W-102.5.1

here in the illusion is attachment and neediness. Love is the energy we receive from God and which we extend out to our world. It is not coming FROM anyone or anything in the outer world.

The people we say we love are the objects of our affection. The ego tells us that these people are the cause of our love and joy. It is God's Love that we are feeling for our loved ones and this we can never lose.

The ego loves to associate love with loss. The more we love someone or something the more the ego pushes our *loss button*. It may be fear of loss of the other, or fear of loss of ourselves.

Let's begin to allow the loving message of this lesson to be the truth that sets us free of our fear of love and allow the joy of love to be evident in our lives for all to see. We are here to be the *Light Workers*.

Let's be the highest example of Love for others to follow. What Joy!!

Lesson 104
"I seek but what belongs to me in truth."

"I seek but what belongs to me in truth."

"In truth," these are the operative words. Guilt, fear, pain, loneliness, etc. are not ours in truth. They are figments of an imagination guided by the ego mind. It is astonishing that we need book after book, speaker after speaker, guidance after guidance to convince us that God Wills His Creation to be happy and peaceful. This shows how powerful, although not real, the ego's messages have been in the world of illusion. We fear joy and love more than we fear the pitiful lives we have invented.

I know it is not easy to completely accept this message when there are experiences going on in our lives that are not joyful and loving, but these are the times when our mind must keep the truth in the forefront. No matter what is happening, if we will keep repeating ideas such as those expressed in today's lesson, the Will of God will become evident in our lives. There is a lesson that tells us to first say the truth often, then to be accepted as partly true with many reservations and finally to be accepted as the truth. This is the practice for us now. We must do this for the Awakening of the world. If not us, who?

God's gifts of peace and joy are the desire of everyone. Let's show the way for this to be experienced in the lives of all.

Lesson 105
"God's peace and joy are mine."

"God's Peace and Joy are mine" can only be experienced as true if we do not deny the same to anyone.

We are all One. Where we withhold the thought of love and peace to anyone, we are not in alignment with God. Thus we cannot have this experience ourselves. God's Peace and Joy are the inheritance of everyone or of no one. If we were to wish to withhold the gift of peace and joy to our so-called *enemies* and think this has an effect on them, we would have to hold the thought that others can do so to us.

We are all the Beloved Children of God, entitled to all His gifts all the time. To withhold accepting the right of anyone to receive God's Gifts separates out part of the Sonship as worthy and other parts as not. This would be denying our Oneness and that IS the original cause of the illusion.

God is no respecter of persons. Thus we realize that we only give to ourselves, since our thoughts do not leave our own minds. If we are thinking that anyone deserves less than God's Will for him or her, it is our mind that suffers. The last sentence in this lesson says it all.

"My brother, peace and joy I offer you, that I may have God's peace and joy as mine." (ACIM)[31]

---

[31] W-105.9.6

Lesson 106
"Let me be still and listen to the truth."

Again, how simple is the instruction in today's lesson. Be still and listen.

We are not asked to memorize complicated prayers, or to read book after book or to do anything at all but be still. We have been given everything we need in our Creation and in order to experience this we must disregard the ego mind that guides us to think we need to get more and more. It tells us that getting is the way to peace. The ego guides us thus: if and when I get the next bauble that is held out to me, then I will be peaceful. How many times do we have to see this fail in our experience until we are ready to give up the control and allow the Voice for God tell us the truth about ourselves?

In this lesson, Jesus is asking us to be still and hear our Father's Voice, then bring this into our world. In the giving of truth, we will know we have it. To give away is to know that we possess it. Most of us have had the experience of talking with others about our experiences with truth, only to realize that in the sharing, the truth becomes more real for us. We give to receive. The ego would have us believe the opposite. We know that there is no need to seek for the truth.

We have only to accept it and share it, and it will manifest in our lives in all good ways.

Lesson 107
"Truth will correct all errors in my mind."

Again, I suggest you read this lesson in its entirety. It is so beautiful that this made it very difficult for me to choose a portion of it to share with you.

"*Truth will correct all errors in my mind*" and bring us happiness beyond measure. What is the Truth that we are being asked to accept? It is simply and wonderfully that we remain as we were created. We were created One with our Father and each other. We are not the physical body, but the Beautiful Loving Energy that animates this body. *It is not I but the Christ within who does the work.*

If we would just release the need to think we are self-made and self-sufficient, and allow the Truth of our Being to be our constant thought, there is nothing here in the illusion that would come near our dwelling place.

As our loving Course tells us, I am One Self united with my Creator and at One with every aspect of Creation, limitless in power and in peace. *Limitless in power and in peace.* Just let this in. This is the truth that will correct error thought and allow this time to be experienced as heaven on earth.

The Course says to be in the Kingdom is merely to focus your full attention on it. How simple is salvation and what bliss this brings with it!!!

Lesson 108
"To give and to receive are one in truth."

If we were to really, really get this lesson, it would seem that we would be more vigilant about becoming aware of our thoughts.

The message would certainly help us to stop judging and blaming others. If we all understood that what we think of others is what we are giving to ourselves, what a different world this would be. This lesson teaches us the fundamental law of cause and effect. You think a thought about yourself or anyone and YOU get the effect.

The ego would have us believe that our thoughts are weakening the one we judge, but this is not the case. How we have misunderstood the laws of mind! To give and to receive are one in truth.

From this moment forward, ask the Holy Spirit to help you become aware of your thoughts, and to help you Think the Thoughts of God. The truth in this lesson can be an eye-opener to many people who think that God is the originator of the ills of the world. Would God give pain unto Itself? What freedom and power there is in the teaching of this lesson. One needs only to try it out to see its effects.

To every one of you I offer beauty and peace and love and joy and freedom and abundance. I wait quietly and confidently as these gifts are returned to me.

Lesson 109
"I rest in God."

At the risk of sounding like a broken record, please read this lesson in its entirety. It is so comforting.

How loving Jesus is to us. Time and time again he teaches us the way to peace of mind. It should be obvious to us by now that peace is not found in the frantic thinking of the world, but somehow this is where we go when events occur that frighten us. From this day forward, let us be willing to learn to allow the thought of resting in God to be our first thought, when the ego threatens our peace with thoughts of the past and/or future.

We rest in the Present Moment, we surrender, we trust and we rest. As we practice this more and more, we will begin to see that most of what the ego frightens us with will never happen… that what is happening, is happening for us, not to us. It is all about healing our mind. From this standpoint, we can rest and watch from a place of peace and power as the ego stories play out.

Lesson 110
"I am as God created me."

We can see the importance of the message of this lesson in the fact that it is repeated so often.

First of all, that there is only One Creator must be established. Either God is the Authority in our mind or each one of us is in charge of making up the story of our lives.

The ego would have us believe that we are victims of the beliefs of the world. It obscures the fact that it is only the ego that can suffer and die. The ego would have us believe that life is a struggle and then we die. How foolish and cruel are the lies of the ego.

We remain as the One Creator wills us to be. We are whole and complete and full of joy. This is the Will of the One Who is expressing Itself as the Christ. But, as we know, the ego's voice speaks loudly and speaks first. It is only in the Silence of our Mind that the Truth can dawn on us.

Let us practice the idea for today. Should any thought, word or symptom come to our attention that would dispute this, let us call upon the Holy Spirit to correct it. We say willingly and lovingly, "Holy Spirit, I invite you into this thought." In this way, the blocks to love's presence are permanently removed from the mind. "*I am as God created me.*"

"This is the key that opens up the gate of Heaven, and lets you enter in the peace of God and His eternity." (ACIM)[32] *The prodigal has returned at last.*

Lesson 111
"Morning and evening review: lessons 91 & 92."

Please read the introduction to this series of lessons for complete instructions on how to work with these lessons.

Only the Vision of the Holy Spirit can give us the Light in which to recognize the Love of God, for that is What we are. If we are thinking from the ego, darkness abounds. It is this darkness of the ego that causes us to feel fearful and vulnerable. The Love Light of the Holy Spirit reveals our True Identity, in which we know we are loved and strong.

When going through the many ego episodes of our life, let us remember, nothing can be solved through ego thinking because the ego sees nothing truly. It is like a child in a dark room seeing shadows and thinking they are monsters. We are the Light. Let our thinking come from a place of Truth. Only then will strength be experienced by us. If you find yourself enmeshed in ego

---

[32] W-110.11.7

thinking, reach out and join with someone or meditate on a thought from the Course. The ego cannot prevail when two are joined in truth."

I need but turn to God and every sorrow melts away, as I accept His boundless Love for me."(ACIM)[33]

Lesson 112
"Morning and evening review: lessons 93 & 94."

Our lesson today is helping us to live consciously in the Kingdom of God here on earth.

We are reminded that the thoughts of the material world are not the Thoughts of God. Unless we practice the Thoughts of God on a regular basis, we will not live our lives from the standpoint of light and joy and peace. We will use our mind to decide what in the world must change before We can experience life from this vantage-point.

Let us, from this day forward, consciously and with all the willingness that we are capable of, remember that we remain as we were created. We are Infinite, Powerful and Loving Beings guided by Wisdom and Love.

In this way, we will become the embodiment of, Thou seeth me, Thou seeth the Father.

Lesson 113
"Morning and evening review: lessons 95 & 96."

Our dear brother Jesus is again reminding us that we cannot change what God has created.

It is God's Kingdom and it remains as He created it to be. We are one Self, not the false self, we imagine ourselves to be AND the Real Self we truly are.

The ego would have us believe that we somehow have changed

---

[33] W-207.1.3

our Identity and are now trying to reclaim it. If we are to understand ourselves, from the Truth of our Being, life would be experienced in a totally different way. I am one Self and that Self is as God created It. Let's take a stand today that in all perceptions of others and ourselves, we start from the Thought of God.

In this way, we will experience ourselves in the Garden of God eternally as was intended.

Lesson 114
"Morning and evening review: lessons 97 & 98."

I love the line, "What can be my function be but to accept the Word of God, Who created me for what I am and will forever be."

How simple and how obvious is the truth. Why would we fight against the Word of the One Who created us? The one who originates something is the one who knows what it is. Even in this illusion this holds true. One must trust the inventor of an invention for what it is and what its function is meant to be. So let us think of ourselves as God assures us we are. God knows this!!! The ego does not know it. Why would we fight God's view of us? God sees us as perfect as It sees Itself.

Let us today stand willing to give up our false concept of what we are, and how sick and sad we can be, and listen to our teacher, Jesus, when he said Follow Me.

Let's follow the teachings of Jesus and awaken and be glad.

Lesson 115
"Morning and evening review: lessons 99 & 100."

As we know, the Course uses the word "salvation" to mean happiness and forgiveness.

It is no wonder that these three words are used interchangeably.

If we are to save ourselves from the ego's guidance, forgiveness is the only means and happiness is the result. So we can restate the title of lesson 99 as forgiveness and happiness are my only functions here. And the ideas in lesson 100, doing my forgiveness work and the resulting happiness, are essential to God's plan.

When we think about it in this way we can experience a new sense of importance as we work on healing our own minds. When we are healed we are not healed alone. God needs us to be an instrument for bringing all of us back to the memory of God. When we allow the *"blocks to the awareness of love's presence, which is your natural inheritance,"*$_{(ACIM)}$[34] to be given to the Holy Spirit, we can truly see ourselves as ministers of God as the Course teaches.

Let us remind ourselves that whatever is a disturbance to our peace today is part of the Great Awakening. We cannot experience our lives as a happy dreamland, and then awaken into Reality with ego beliefs and concepts still part of our mind. The Thoughts of God are our Real Thoughts.

As we practice, allowing only these to be real for us, we are accepting God's plan for the Great Awakening.

Lesson 116
"Morning and evening review: lessons 101 & 102."

If we were to practice these lessons in our lives on a daily basis, our only thought in all circumstances would be "Thy Will be done."

We must look in our minds and search out any thoughts that conflict with this idea. "Thy Will" is only happiness, peace, joy, abundance, wholeness, freedom and beauty. What could we desire here in this illusionary world that does not come under one of these headings!!

---

[34] Introduction.1.7

From now on let us not pray for things of this world. They do not last and the ego will rob us of the joy of them. Pray only for what God wills for us. Pray for content, not form. Trust that God will overflow His Will in areas where we may feel a need. And so we will begin to have the experience that one of the Miracles Principles expresses: Miracles are natural.

"Miracles are natural, and when they do not occur something has gone wrong."(ACIM)[35] And what has gone wrong is that we may be thinking thoughts that are not in alignment with the Thoughts of God. To line up our thoughts we simply have to surrender our need to control and to trust the Will of God in all ways.

How joyous it is to know that God's Will is done and everyone is happy.

Lesson 117
"Morning and evening review: lessons 103 & 104."

How sad it is that we have wandered so from the belief that God=Love=Joy!

For me, it happened when I was a very young girl and the story of the crucifixion was told to me. The words of Jesus in the Garden of Gethsemane struck fear in my heart for a long time. I was taught that Jesus supposedly prayed the night before the crucifixion was to take place. Something to the effect of, *Father if it is possible, let this cup pass from me, not as I will but as Thou wilt*. We all know what happened to him after this.

From then on, until I did my inner work with the teachings of the Course, "*Thy will be done*" was not a comforting prayer. However, as I listened to Jesus discuss this event in the Course, I realized how misunderstood the whole story of the crucifixion was.

Possibly it would be helpful to look deep within yourself and see if there is still some lingering belief that God is somewhat

---

[35] T-9.IV.6.2

fearful. I am sure that by now this idea has been healed for you, but there still may be some semblance of old beliefs lurking in your holy mind. If so, give it to Holy Spirit to forgive and heal for you.

Now it is time for us to practice the idea that *God being Love, is also happiness.* God is love and love brings happiness and happiness is our Divine Inheritance. If we are truly to believe the Course when it says *"God wills you learn what always has been true: that He created you as part of Him, and this must still be true because **ideas leave not their source.**"*$_{(ACIM)}$[36] Ideas do not leave their Source.

We must realize that God being Love and Happiness could not extend anything but this to Its Creation. M

Lesson 118
"Morning and evening review: lessons 105 & 106."

It must be obvious by now that the lessons are trying to break the world's way of thinking and bringing us to the truth.

God loves us. God wants us to be happy. Stop for a moment and think of a circumstance in your life and apply this thought to it. The next step is for us to be vigilant not to let our *feeble voice* obscure the truth. Surely, the ego's voice does not seem feeble when it is reciting its ritual of fear thoughts.

We are as God created us, unlimited in power and peace. Therefore, when we realize our true Identity, the ego's voice has little effect on us. The main part we must play is to be vigilant as to which voice is guiding us. When fear thoughts come to mind, be aware that this is not the Voice of God. God's Voice is unlimited in power and peace. It is the Voice for the Father that we honor today, not our own (ego) wisdom.

We have the Wisdom of the Creator available to us, and it is only this we choose from now on.

---

[36] T-26.VII.13.2

Lesson 119
"Morning and evening review: lessons 107 & 108."

What good news to learn that we were mistaken when we believed that we were sinners and worthy of guilt and pain.

No matter what we have done, or what we have not done, we are still His Beloved in Whom He is well pleased. This lesson is telling us that in order for us to experience this, we must forgive all things. Whatever it is that we may be holding against a person, place or thing is the block to the awareness of our true Identity as the Beloved of God.

We receive as we give and if we are giving an interpretation of something other than what God sees, this is what we see in ourselves. Thus, we must realize that God only sees us as peaceful and powerful since that is what is in the Mind of God. God can only give what It is. When this is the way we think about our world, the Love of God will be experienced in the forms that will bring joy to our lives.

Lesson 120
"Morning and evening review: lessons 109 & 110."

Unceasingly, the sages of the ages have advised us to surrender all to God.

If we would only trust the Loving and all Giving Energy of our Creator, we would surely not have any difficulty in surrendering all to God. The ego has given us such a misguided picture of our Father that trusting in God has become very fearful.

Usually it is only when the situation is so out of control or the pain has become extremely strong that we finally *Rest in God*. Let us practice today using the words from our Course. *"I rest in God today, and let Him work in me and through me, while I rest in Him in quiet and in perfect certainty."* As we let this be a day of complete surrender, we will know from its results the joy and peace of trusting the One Who Created. Thus, we will come to know Ourselves as God meant us to be.

The Lessons Illuminated
Lessons & Review of ACIM 121-180

TRUST, SWEET TRUST,
brings us the peace of God. To know that we do not know is the
highest place we can be spiritually

Illustrated by Cathleen Schott

Lesson 121
"Forgiveness is the key to happiness."

This is a mighty lesson. Please read the entire lesson when you have the willingness.

The first line in this lesson says it all. *"Here is the answer to your search for peace."* As we know, in peace were we created and in peace we remain. Yet at times we feel anything but peace. Well, this lesson is giving us the reason. We are holding a thought in our holy mind that is not a Thought of God.

If we are to experience our *True Identity*, which is the only way to the Peace of God, we must think as our Creator intended. We are not meant to hold grievances, judgments, or blame against anyone or ourselves. It is only through the alignment of our energy with the Energy of God that true peace is experienced.

What a small price to pay for all the Good of the Universe. Release the need to be right that something is wrong with you or anyone. No matter what the appearance, we are still as God created us.

As we remember this, peace is inevitable.

Lesson 122
"Forgiveness offers everything I want."

Each time I do this lesson, it makes me think that if this were to be a commercial for a new product, there would be a rush to purchase it!

Re-read the above and allow yourself the whimsy of imagining this as something that has been discovered in the material world that could guarantee you what it offers. This is the *product* that the Holy Spirit is offering to us *for free*. We know that it is effective from our own experience. What is it within us that needs continual repeating about this offer from the Holy Spirit? The only answer that the Course gives us is that we think we need to be right.

The ego mind creates a perception about someone/something that it is possible our peace, love and joy can be taken from us. We would rather be right, that this perception is possible, than have the Peace of God. What a poor trade we make.

"Forgiveness offers everything I want." Let's start by forgiving ourselves.

Lesson 123
"I thank my Father for His gifts to me."

While meditating and using the suggestion of 15 minutes spent in gratitude, there appeared to me a long pathway.

In the process of looking at my past, I saw symbolized all the events of my life that happened up until now. The path seemed to be strewn with branches, rocks and holes and many other obstacles, and also beautiful flowers and trees. As I walked along this path, I saw through each healing event, that I was not alone. My Real Self was with me, and alongside me were angels and helpers. The feeling of gratitude that came over me was wonderful. Then, I noticed that the path ahead was obscured to me at this time. I could see a shining Glow, lighting the rest of the way. What peace washed over me?

I hope that by sharing this with you it will give you a *visual* to enter into your time of gratitude. We do not walk alone. God's Angels hover near and all about us. Of this we can be sure; *"He would not leave you **comfortless**, alone in dreams of hell, but would release your mind from everything that hides His face from you."* (ACIM)[37]

And so, we can seemingly move forward in this dream of separation, holding in mind our gratitude for only happy outcomes. Forget not that the healing of our mind is all the world is for and we do not do this alone.

We are happy and grateful that this is so. Thank you, Dear God.

---

[37] T-31.VIII.3.5

Lesson 124
"Let me remember I am one with God."

Here we are with another lesson in gratitude for what is the Truth.

We are one with God. Once this has been experienced there is nothing else to say. But for now, our lesson guides us ever so gently to the place of full awareness of our True Identity. One of the many things I love about our Course is that it never pressures us to receive the Truth that it is offering to us.

There are several places in this lesson that say "*perhaps today, perhaps tomorrow.*" As it says in the Introduction to the Text, "*only the time you take it is voluntary.*" Our dear brother Jesus understands the level of unconsciousness that some of us are experiencing, and he is offering us a spark of Light. This spark will eventually burst into the Great Rays of Divine Awareness of Who we truly are.

We are asked only to be willing to have this experience by practicing what the lessons are sharing with us.

Gently, ever so gently, "we go our way rejoicing, with the thought that God Himself goes everywhere with us," (ACIM)[38] And with the full awareness that we are one with God and each other.

Lesson 125
"In quiet I receive God's Word today."

Again, it was very difficult for me to select which parts of this lesson to share. The lesson is filled with gems.

I began this lesson by repeating the title several times, and then I waited to hear God's Words to me. I did this as one would when speaking to another person. First, we speak and then we await their answer. I felt that repeating the title of this lesson several times was my invitation to God to share His Loving Thoughts

---
[38] W-124.1.5

with me.

Even the act of listening is powerful in itself. It is an indication that we *know* the Father is speaking to us and that we are willing to hear. At times, one does not seem to hear anything, but most of us will hear some words of Truth. As we hear these words, we notice that they bring comfort and peace with them. From here it becomes easier and easier to find the time and willingness to quiet our minds and listen. Just be quiet and listen and enjoy the love and insights that emerge.

The thoughts of the world take no effort to hear. It is God's Voice that requires quietness. For me, when I am thinking the ego's/world's thoughts, it seems that I am talking to myself; what if this, what if that, how could they, recounting past experiences and conversations.

However, as I stop this stream of meaningless thoughts and just wait and listen, a sense of stillness that is so familiar and loving comes over me, and now I am with my God, loved and loving. As this communion with God is experienced on a regular basis, it seems that, it becomes more and more difficult to return to the world's way of thinking.

Excuse me now, I feel called to return to this quietness. Love, Love, Love.

Lesson 126
"All that I give is given to myself."

Most of us who have been studying Truth are aware of this principle. It is good to have a deep review of the topic.

We know that when we judge, we suffer and when we love, we are peaceful. This is the simplicity of salvation. The world thinks in terms of material things. In this sense, when we give something away, it surely seems that we do not have it any longer. However, the Course always refers to ideas. Thus, we can better understand today's lesson.

When I think thoughts from the ego mind, I am in fear. When I think the Thoughts of God, I am peaceful. In these days of political and other unrest in the world, it is important that we are vigilant in what we are thinking and saying about those we seem to oppose. Peaceful thoughts about those running for office, of any persuasion, are *gifts* we give to ourselves. We are well aware that many of our political stances are upsetting us. But, it takes commitment to truth to realize that it is only our thoughts that are upsetting us, not what he or she is saying or doing. Our thoughts alone can cause us pain or joy.

So, we come back to the title of this lesson, *"all that I give is given to myself."* I am giving myself joy or pain through my thoughts about situations in my life. Let's agree to be more vigilant about what we think and say, knowing that these ideas do not leave our own mind. As this lesson reminds us Help is available to us at all times. Let us trust in God's Help, moment to moment, in the healing of our minds.

We now allow the Power and Glory of our Oneness with our Father and each other to return to our awareness.

Lesson 127
"There is no love but God's."

The first sentences from several of the paragraphs seem to come together to give us a picture of what our dear Jesus is teaching us.

In the world of form, there is little that we understand about the meaning of true love. The simple truth is that we ARE Love. When we are not extending love, we feel guilty. The guilt we feel is simply the result of the decision not to love.

We are not angry or sad because of what someone has done or not done, we are always upset because we have entertained the thought, *now I can't love you*. It is this thought that brings us pain because it is not natural to us. *"You have denied the condition of his being, which is his perfect blamelessness. Out of love he was created, and in love he abides."* (ACIM)[39]

---

[39] T-13.I.6.5&6

Let us today ask the Holy Spirit and Jesus to give us an experience of love anytime we are tempted to withhold the love that we are. It is the withholding of Ourselves that brings us pain. We allow Infinite Love to fill our mind and look through eyes of love at all we see in the world of form. In this way, we ensure our own sense of peace and joy.

"The opposite of love is fear, but what is all-encompassing can have no opposite."(ACIM)[40]

Lesson 128
"The world I see holds nothing that I want."

There is little doubt that most of us have experienced the truth of the message of this lesson.

How many times have we thought, when this problem is solved, I will be happy! Or, when I achieve this or receive that, then I will be happy and peaceful. Most of us have done this over and over and we are probably still thinking this to some extent. However, if we are honest with ourselves, we will realize that as soon as one seeming problem is solved another pops us; or when we have achieved our desired goal, another bauble is held out before us. We never seem to *arrive* as we seek the things the world holds as good.

If we look to content and not to form, we can always have our true desire. Our true and only desire is the Peace of God. If we were to honestly look at any desire in this world, we would see that the real thought is *then I will be peaceful*.

Let's begin today to let this lesson do its mighty work, and help us to withdraw our attachment to the things of this world, and accept what we truly desire. There is nothing required of us to have this, but the willingness to be as God created us.

God created us in peace and love and joy and in this we remain.

---

[40] Introduction.1.8

Lesson 129
"Beyond this world there is a world I want."

With this lesson we are being led to understand that there is only one world and that is the world of our Almighty Father.

The world we seem to see has never satisfied us, but there is a world that holds everything we want. However, first we must accept that there are not really two worlds. The one is an illusion, meaningless in all its ways, and does not exist except in our imaginations. We are One with God in His Creation. This is the only world that holds our desires fulfilled forever and ever. This is the world we want.

The ego has many ingenious ways of tricking us into believing we can find the joys of God's World here in form, but as we said yesterday, this has not and will not ever happen. The ego guides us to believe that control and defense and attack will bring us the Peace of God. We all know how well this has worked.

Let us now surrender to the fact that wherever we are, God is, and that, knowing our True Identity will bring to us all good and only good as is intended. We accept that God and I are One and GOD is that One. It is God's world for which we have searched, but in all the wrong places, only to find it waiting patiently behind every grievance and error thought. The Father and I are One and in this Oneness is the Inheritance we deserve.

This is the world we want. Only this!!

Lesson 130
"It is impossible to see two worlds."

It is always amazing to me that we find it so difficult to give up the world of fear in place of the strength and love of God.

As the years have gone by in my life, I realize more and more how unconscious I have been. The temptation to believe the voice of fear about life's circumstances is so strong, yet it is this we do not want.

Practicing this lesson clearly pointes out the choice to us: Heaven or hell, fear or love, God or the ego. These are the only choices we have in all areas of our lives.

We no longer can claim unconsciousness as our excuse for the pain in our lives. Jesus is laying it out very clearly in this lesson. We are as God created us or we are as we made up what we are. Let us remember that God is the Father/Mother and we are the Child. We are completely protected and provided for by this Loving Parent.

Our part is to surrender our mind to this thought only. *"It is impossible to see two worlds which have no overlap of any kind. Seek for the one; the other disappears."*$_{(ACIM)}$[41]

Choose your world. *"I have set before thee life and death.... therefore choose life,"* [42]

CHOOSE LIFE.....CHOOSE LOVE.....CHOOSE GOD.

Lesson 131
"No one can fail who seeks to reach the truth."

There is so much more to this beautiful lesson. Please try to read it in its entirety.

We who have been studying the truth for so long must accept that we cannot fail to reach the truth. It seems that we get so involved in the searching that we sometimes forget that the journey will end where it began.

The ego guides us to search and search; to talk about the truth endlessly but never to reach it. There is an old joke that says if there were two doors ...one marked *talking about God* and the other marked God, the line would be very long for the *talking* door.

---

[41] W-130.5.1

[42] Deuteronomy 30:19ASV American Standard Version

We can reach the truth today. As we go through this day, let's allow this thought to be with us. We can reach the truth today. Not just talk about it, nor search for it, but reach it because we have never really left it. The searching, that has meaning in this world, is to seek and find the Holy Spirit's guidance in all that we encounter. Through His Vision we will see the truth shining in our mind where it never left.

Here I am Father, accepting Your Grace. I can rest.

Lesson 132
"I loose the world from all I thought it was."

What a practical lesson this is!! It truly lays out the secret of peace and happiness.

There is no absolute world OUT there. The only world we are always dealing with is our inner world of thought and beliefs. If we were only taught this from childhood, what a different world there would be.

We have all had the experience of changing our perception about an event in our lives and seeing THE change that takes place in our experience. I am sure we can think of something that happened in just the last few days to prove this. We live from our core beliefs, and thankfully, these can be changed. However, often we change our beliefs to other beliefs, perhaps more comfortable, but still not the truth.

WE ARE AS GOD CREATED US. If we would just start from this knowingness, and then allow God to work through us in all our adventures here in the body, our lives would reflect the truth. God's Will for us is perfect happiness, and when we surrender the need to think otherwise, this will be evident. Let this day be the day that we give ourselves the gift of returning our will to the Creator. We allow This Perfect Life to flow through us now and forever more.

Thy Will is done. Everyone is happy. Thank you Father/Mother God.

Lesson 133
"I will not value what is valueless."

How lovingly our brother, Jesus, lays out the problem of this ego world.

We seek and find what we do not really value, and then go on to seek another something that will be unwanted when achieved. As we process the steps laid out in this lesson, it becomes obvious that what we really always ever want is the Peace of God. Buried under our wishes and yearnings is the desire for the Peace, which is our Inheritance and our Identity.

We want to consciously know Who we are. We want to feel the Oneness and Joy of our Father's Love. This is the only value here. We are awakening to giving up our sense of autonomy in favor of knowing that it is the Father within Who does the work. And so we let go the valueless in favor of the wonderment that is truly ours. We understand the line from this lesson that states;

"You do not ask too much of life, but far too little."

Lesson 134
"Let me perceive forgiveness as it is."

To get the full gift you may want to read the entire lesson of the day.

Our Course tells us that the way to God is through forgiveness here. There is no other way. Thus we can see how valuable it is to perceive forgiveness as it is. Forgiveness is not understanding, it is not pardon, it is not approval. It is simply allowing our mind to withdraw the judgments that we may have made. It is this judgment that keeps us out of alignment with the Thoughts of God and thus leads to our feelings of fear and guilt.

We think discomfort comes from the appearance that something has occurred that seems unforgivable to us, but it is coming from the fact that we are seeing the event through the eyes of the ego. The ego tells us that we are vulnerable and capable of being hurt, but if we remember that we are as God created us, we would know that this is impossible.

True forgiveness knows that nothing can take the peace of God from us. We can experience something that feels as though we have lost this peace, but it is only our false perceptions that make this so. A simple definition of forgiveness for me is to withdraw my judgment of the situation. As I withdraw the ego judgments, the Love and Light of God is evident once more. It is like a cloudy day in which it appears as though the sun is not shining. When the clouds move away, we see that the sun was there all the time.

We can experience this while on a plane. I think this is a good analogy of what forgiveness is. When we raise our energy above the clouds of ego thinking we find that the loving energy of our Creator was there all the time. To help us forgive what needs to be forgiven, we might ask ourselves the questions that the Course proposes: Do you want to be right or peaceful? Do you want the clouds or the sunshine? It is up to us to choose.

Let us choose peace, and as we do our world will reflect this choice.

Lesson 135
"If I defend myself I am attacked."

Whew!!! The second or third time I did the lessons, I spent about a month working with this lesson. I highly recommend that you spend some time with the Truth here as well.

This lesson is about surrender and trust. Trust is the first characteristic of a Teacher of God. Without trust we cannot let go of the ego identity, to which we so foolishly cling, and allow the awareness of our Identity as the Christ, to return to our holy minds.

Defense and control are the ideas of the ego to give us the peace we seek. We all know how *well* this has worked for us. The more defensive and controlling we become, the more fear we experience. How could we, in our mortal limited mind, know all there is to know about any situation? Any thought we may have accepted from the ego to give us peace, the ego immediately snatched from us.

Our Course says, *"The unforgiving mind is torn with doubt, confused about itself and all it sees; afraid and angry, weak and blustering, **afraid to go ahead, afraid to stay, afraid to waken or to go to sleep**, afraid of every sound, yet more afraid of stillness; terrified of darkness, yet more terrified at the approach of light."* (ACIM)[43]

We get this picture when we try to defend ourselves. Trust, sweet trust, brings us the Peace of God. To know that we do not know is the highest place we can be spiritually. Let this be the day that we live from the thought, God is the Love in which I trust, and I can do all things through God Who guides me. Then we relax and watch the blessings God bestows upon us.

We are willing to be pleasantly surprised. Thank you Father that the Truth is true.

Lesson 136
"Sickness is a defense against the truth."

What an interesting lesson this is!!

Let us remember when Jesus refers to sickness, he is not just referring to physical illness. He is talking about anything in our lives that is not peace and love and joy. This might be in the area of relationships, money, careers, etc., So, as you work with this lesson apply its truth to the area in your own life that may be out of alignment with God's Will for happiness for you.

This lesson teaches, sickness is a magic wand we wave when truth is dawning in our holy mind. This is the distraction the ego uses to keep our mind from knowing that we are as God created

---

[43] W-121.3.1

us, and not as we made ourselves. Let us know that when problems seem to appear in our lives this is the time when we are closest to our miracle. Let us keep our mind focused on the line from our Course that states;

"Behind this is a miracle to which I am entitled. Let me not hold a grievance against you, [name], but offer you the miracle that belongs to you instead. Seen truly, this offers me a miracle."(ACIM)[44]

Lesson 137
"When I am healed I am not healed alone."

While we heal our minds about the body, and thus about our True Identity, there is little doubt that it has an effect on others.

We can only experience the Peace of God when we are aware of our Oneness with God and each other. When we begin to feel tempted by thoughts of illness, of any kind, the ego's advice is always to isolate. There seem to be two reasons for this. One is that in isolation, it is easier for the ego's lies to seem true, and thus delay our healing. The other is that when we are healed of whatever is appearing as sickness, when the miracle occurs it does not seem to benefit anyone but ourselves.

This is not Heaven's Way. The Way of Heaven is sharing and extending. When we stray from this way of being we are more prone to be victims of the ego's suggestions. As the Course teaches, when we are healed we are not healed alone. This blesses the giver and the receiver. When we join with each other in the healing event, healing is strengthened for all. *"Remember that ideas increase only by being shared."*(ACIM)[45] Let's *give away* the Thoughts of God in order to strengthen them in ourselves. We are and always will be as God created us. God is the First Cause and knows us as we are.

As we give up the need to be something else, wholeness occurs for all and us.

---

[44] W-89.2.2-4
[45] T-5.VI.7.1

Lesson 138
"Heaven is the decision I must make."

Heaven is (Oneness, Wholeness, Peace, Love, Joy, Beauty, Freedom, Abundance, to name a few) the decision we must make.

We were taught in lesson 133 a few days ago, to not value what is valueless. I must remind us of the criteria for choice mentioned in this lesson. First, will what you want to last forever? Second, does it take something from someone else? Third, what purpose does it serve? Fourth, do you feel any guilt about your choice? It is so good to be reminded that our only choices are heaven or hell.

If the decisions we feel we must make have many sides to them and lead us to feeling confused and frightened, then we know that we have a complicated the process. Heaven or Hell, Choose! Thus, when life brings to us circumstances for which there seem to be many choices, let's remember that what we really want is Heaven. We want the Peace of God, no matter what else seems to be beckoning to us. The goal of all goals is Heaven.

Whatever it is that you feel would make your life happier or more peaceful right now, please add these words to your thought about it. I seem to want _____, but what I really want is Heaven. We know that the way to Heaven is through forgiveness and love. We cannot lose.

God's Will and ours are united once more. We are Home.

Lesson 139
"I will accept Atonement for myself."

What a fabulous lesson. It is the answer to all the problems and questions we have about this ego world.

You know the questions the ego world raises. How can people act like that? This makes no sense! What is this about? I don't understand how these things happen, and on and on. The reason for it all is that we have forgotten who we truly are. As the saying goes (and I know that you probably all have heard it), we are not humans having a spiritual experience, but spirits having a human experience.

When we remember *Who* we truly are, fear and guilt and lack and greed and judgment become impossible. We would experience ourselves as One with the Whole. What One has, all have.

Let's remember that all of our problems are about our relationship with God, and the Truth of What we are. We are as God created us. We are One with each other and with God and nothing can change the Eternal Love and Grace of our Father. To live from this perspective is the Atonement.

I would like to end with a quote from another lesson in the Workbook. *"What can I seek for, Father, but Your Love? Perhaps I think I seek for something else; a something I have called by many names. Yet is **Your Love the only thing I seek**, or ever sought. For there is nothing else that I could ever really want to find. Let me remember You. What else could I desire but the truth about myself?"* (ACIM)[46]

Lesson 140
"Only Salvation can be said to cure."

Time and again our elder brother Jesus, reminds us that we are as God created us.

And as God created us, sickness, lack, and suffering of any kind is impossible. It does not exist in the Mind of God and was not extended to our minds in our Creation. God came first and filled all space. *All Space!* There is not a spot where God is not. Can we imagine God suffering from a backache, headache, money problem, or relationship issue? Of course not! God is, Eternal Joyous Spirit, and we are created in His Image and Likeness.

Practicing the truth about ourselves is the only cure that exists. Everything else is a temporary measure. It is similar to putting a

---

[46] W-231.1. 1-6

Band-Aid on the issue only to have the Band-Aid fall off revealing the problem once more. God is Eternal Wholeness.

The wholeness problem can be solved by *not* following the ego guidance that tells us we are guilty and not worthy. The last line of this lesson says, *"This is the day when separation ends, and we remember Who we really are."*

Today we allow God's Will to appear in our lives as peace and love and joy for evermore.

Lesson 141
"Review of Lessons 121 & 122."

The lessons we are working with for this review are only one line long. I will be sharing a thought a day from the section that introduces these lessons.

The only way to become aware that our mind holds only what we think with God, is to disregard the thoughts the ego has inculcated in our minds. We were not created to be fearful or guilty or lacking of any goodness. It is only through forgiveness (which is the releasing of the ego judgments) that the Light and Love of our Father will be revealed to us once more.

Let's review the titles of the lessons mentioned above and contemplate the truth of these reminders. We are readying our minds for the lessons to come. As we are vigilant in our practice, we allow ourselves to shift to an even higher level of consciousness. Be still and ask yourself this question: "Am I really willing to have my mind hold only what I think with God?" At first glance, one would say yes, but let's dig deep and look at what may block us from accepting this into our mind. We will be asked to release all grievances and judgments against others and ourselves and to remain in the *Now Moment*. We must be vigilant in our awareness of our thoughts. When a thought arises that is not a *Thought of God,* we must immediately say, *Holy Spirit I invite you into this thought,* or any other idea that will bless you. *Let's go for it. It is time for us to have our Divine Inheritance. Now is the only time there is. Now is the time for us to remember Home.*

Lesson 142
"Review of Lessons 123 & 124."

When we work with the review of these lessons, let's contemplate what it truly means when it reminds us.

"There is a central theme that unifies each step in the review we undertake which can be simply stated in these words: **My mind holds only what I think with God**. *That is a fact, and represents the truth of What you are and What your Father is.*" (ACIM)[47]

There can be all sorts of thoughts that come and go in our holy mind but no matter what, our mind HOLDS only God's Thoughts. Under all the ego madness in which we sometimes dwell for a time, God remains. There is a saying that I often share at our meetings: *God came first and fills all space.* There is not one spot where God is not. Thus, through the grace of God, His Presence is never lost to us. We thank our Father that this is true, now and always, and with this gratitude comes the full awareness that God and I are One and God is that One.

We relax in the comfort of the everlasting Peace and Love of God. This is what is held in the mind of all forever.

Lesson 143
"Review of Lessons 125 & 126."

While I meditated today on the following words from the lesson; "*In quiet I receive God's Word today*," I realized that *God's Word* does not refer to the words that we use to communicate with each other here in the illusion. God's Word comes as an experience of the essence of God. It may come in the experience of joy or peace or love, or any of the attributes of God. It is we ourselves that convert this energy into words that comfort us. God's Energy is so natural to us that from this place of our true Identity, all questions are answered. All requests are granted in the perfect form at the perfect time.

---

[47] W-Review IV Introduction 2.1&2

Let us today quiet our ego yammering, and allow the quietness to be revealed in our mind, so that we may receive what it is we truly desire. God is our heart's desire, only God. It is only when the ego mind is quieted that we experience this Presence, although it is always with us.

"I rest in God. This thought will bring to you the rest and quiet, peace and stillness, and the safety and the happiness you seek." (ACIM)[48]

Lesson 144
"Review of Lessons 127 & 128."

"My mind holds only what I think with God."

What heavenly news this is. Thoughts that we believe are judging, attacking and unkind do not exist in our holy mind. Only loving thoughts are eternal. These are the thoughts that come from our Father and belong to His Creation. Oh yes, there are those other thoughts that come and go through our minds. But, their energy is so weak that they blow away like clouds on a windy day, unless we generate them repeatedly.

The world we see holds nothing that we want and these other thoughts always involve the world we see. Someone says or does something (or does not say or do something) and we relentlessly go over it in our minds. When we are willing to allow the Love of God to be the only *thought energy* in our mind, then we realize how foolish we were to have been so attached to thoughts that do not line up with This energy.

"There is no Love but God's, and all of love is His." (ACIM)[49] This is the content of our wanting here. We want the Love of God, and it is available to us at all times waiting under the senseless musing with which we entertain ourselves. We want the Love of God. It is not found in the world we see, no matter how wonderful this world may seem. It is found in our Soul and from here we look out on a world blessed with Truth.

---

[48] W-109.2.1&2
[49] W-127.3.5

How beautiful the world becomes when seen from this vantage point, how peaceful and how loving.

Lesson 145
"Review of Lessons 129 & 130."

How little is asked of us in exchange for so much.

We are asked to allow our mind to hold only the Thoughts of God for five minutes, and in exchange God's gifts return to our awareness for the day. We know that God's World is our heart's desire. It is the only thing that gives us lasting satisfaction and joy. However, again and again, we seem to be seduced by the things in the form world. Let's use the message in this lesson today to transcend the temptations of the world we see and remember that it is God's World that we want.

Further, the message in this lesson is that "*It is impossible to see two worlds.*" However, let us remember seeking first the Kingdom of God brings all good things into our experience. The Love of God will overflow into all areas of our lives that need to be healed and we will experience Heaven here on earth.

Thy Will be done on earth as it is in Heaven. Amen

Lesson 146
"Review of Lessons 131 & 132."

How wonderful it will be when we completely loose the world from all we think it is!!

When this has occurred, there will be nothing but Heaven on earth. The Great Awakening will have taken place and nothing but God's Will will be done. How wonderful to know that no one can fail to reach this state of consciousness. When we have pmoment and with a sigh, remember, *"And you will think, in glad astonishment, that **for all this you gave up nothing!** The joy of Heaven, which has no limit, is increased with each light that returns to take its rightful place within it."* (ACIM)[50]

Ahhhhhhh, God, Hello, we're Home.

Lesson 147
"Review of Lessons 133 & 134."

At the time that I meditated today on the title of lesson 133, *"I will not value what is valueless"*, I realized how each of the review lessons lines up with the main message of this section of the Workbook, *"My mind holds only what I think with God."*

If this is true for us, we certainly would not value the valueless thoughts that the ego suggests to us. The idea of judgment, control, blame, sickness, painful relationships, etc., would be laughable to us. Who in their Right Mind would want to entertain such foolish ideas when the Power and the Glory of God is available to us! We would indeed perceive forgiveness as it is because there would be nothing to forgive. All unforgiving thoughts merely disappear, never to appear again, as the Love of God fills our minds.

Father, reveal yourself to me. Reveal your purpose for my life. I am yours.

Lesson 148
"Review of Lessons 135 & 136."

When we agree to allow our mind to hold only what we think with God, there is little doubt that defense, attack and sickness will not exist for us.

When we know Who walks with us, attack and defense become useless. Sickness will disappear from our mind, body and affairs. When we have completely accepted that GOD is the Mind with which we think, and that attack and defense have no energy to sustain themselves, then sickness becomes a thing of the past. Sickness (or lack of God's Goodness in any form) is a symptom that we have misused our mind, and allowed guilt to enter.

---

[50] T-16.VI.11.4&5

Let us today bring to the Altar anything in our lives that would block the awareness that we are in Heaven right now. We surrender the belief in guilt, deprivation, and abandonment and allow these thoughts to return to the nothingness from which they came. They do not belong to us. We are of God and God fills all space. There is nowhere that these beliefs fit into God's Idea of Creation. God's Mind is our mind, and our mind is God's Mind.

Let's join in this thought, I no longer grant anything not of God to have any power over me. Amen.

Lesson 149
"Review of Lessons 137 & 138."

At this point in our studies I am sure we realized the consequence of what we practice.

There is nothing more important in our lives than to heal our mind of ego thinking and allow our minds to hold only what we think with God. As the review lesson mentions, when we are healed we are not healed alone.

Each time we release the need to be right about thinking there is something wrong with ourselves or anyone else, the path to the Great Awakening becomes brighter and easier. What could be of greater significance than to remember Who we truly are?

Let us today be vigilant in our thinking, and honor the work we are doing in the healing of our minds. We do this not just for ourselves, but also for all who falsely believe in the separation of God's Son from the Father. We joyfully make the decision for Heaven today in *all* our thoughts, words and deeds.

We are Earth Angels sent here to help with the Awakening of the planet. If not us, who?

Lesson 150
"Review of Lessons 137 & 138."

I love how Holy Spirit works through us to show us how protected and provided for we are.

While practicing the lesson for today, keep in mind the blessings that are ours, while we raise our consciousness to the level of gratitude and love, to and from our Creator. We accept Atonement for ourselves and so we are bringers of salvation to the world around us and beyond.

The Course tells us that we have no idea how far-reaching the effect of our spiritual work actually is. People we do not know are blessed, as we are blessed, by the spiritual work of others. The only requirement is the willingness to be in alignment with our Loving Father.

I suggest that as we move forward with our study of the lessons, we allow ourselves to daily remember that our mind holds only what we think with God. And as other thoughts try to intrude, we will be conscious of what is in the mind of God and what is not. And so we go rejoicing in the endless love of God for us and for all.

Thank you Father/Mother God for your everlasting Love and Grace.

Lesson 151
"All things are echoes of the Voice for God."

While working with this lesson today, the realization came to me how urgent it is for us to practice the truth in our Course.

This time in history could well be the dawning of the Great Awakening. I feel it is, as do so many other people. The practice of the truth is more important than ever. We are the ministers of God, just think about this. We are bringers of the awareness of the Love of God to this tired and sad world. It is almost breathtaking.

Jesus is asking us to surrender the power that the things of this world hold over our minds and to release our mind to the Voice for God. There is no sacrifice in this. We give pain, suffering, and sadness in glad exchange for peace and love and joy and so much more. The only price asked of us is the little willingness to release the need to be right about what we see and hear.

We are Spirit. Spirituality is invisible. Let us, today, take the pledge to allow the Voice for God to be our final authority in all areas of our lives. As we live the spiritual life, the world's thirst for peace will be quenched along with ours.

Father we listen for Your Voice, and give it to Your Children. Speak to us, our Father. Your beloved listens.

Lesson 152
"The power of decision is my own."

The message of this lesson is so simple.

It can be hidden in the many words contained within. But, the only thing we need to glean from it is that truth is true and nothing else is true. The truth is that we are one with God. We came from God and in God do we remain.

The frantic madness that we have made seems so real, but has been nothing but the arrogance of ego thinking. God says we are perfect, and the ego has us believe we are guilty sinners. God says we are whole and complete and full of joy, and the ego says we are sick and lonely and in pain. Choose what is the truth and what are lies. This is the decision that we must make. Determine today that God is right and that we are wrong about Who we are.

Let this be the day we awaken and return to God.

Lesson 153
"In my defenselessness my safety lies."

How wonderful to know that we do not walk alone in this crazy illusion. We have no need to be afraid when we know Who walks with us.

Of course, the problem is that we get so caught up in the ego's suggestions of fear and attack and defense, that we do not hear the Holy Spirit's Voice telling us *I am here*. To become aware, we must first quiet our mind enough to hear this gentle loving energy. It is like trying to hear a dear friend talk to us amid a noisy crowd.

I suggest, when we get caught up in the defense *game,* we remind ourselves to silently say STOP. Say this aloud if appropriate. We thus take our power back, and stop the stream of the ego's reminders of a painful past, and/or its invitations to believe in a fearful future. This will bring us back to the Now moment where we are safe in the Arms of God.

In the beginning we may have to practice quieting our mind quite often. Eventually we ignore the ego's dictates, and listening to the Holy Spirit will become as natural as breathing. When this becomes habit, the defense and attack thoughts of the past will become almost a laughable solution to any situation.

God's Voice holds the answer to all questions and perceived problems. The more we trust this; our present happiness will be our only experience.

When we realize that trust in the Holy Spirit is our strength, this lifetime becomes the happy game to which this lesson refers. Here is a thought that I often use when I become afraid, and the temptation to attack or defend presents itself to my holy mind:

Present trust equals future joy.

Lesson 154
"I am among the ministers of God."

This is another powerful and loving message from our Brother, Jesus. How lovely is the spiritual life. There is nothing that we can give away except that it blesses us.

In order to be a messenger of God, we must be healed healers. The message that we receive from the Holy Spirit to give to the world is first meant to heal our own ego errors. It is obvious when someone is sharing hollow words from the Course or any other spiritual path. The words sound flat and without energy. However, when one has received the message from our Teacher and applied it to their own lives first, their words take on a power and glory.

To be a true minister of God, we must listen to the things we say to others and know that the message is for us first. When we truly receive the message, then it is ours to share with the world. It is profoundly meaningful to be an instrument of peace for our sisters and brothers. But, to do so, we must feel the peace of God ourselves.

Father, we accept Your Wisdom and Your Love. And, as we go into our lives, we allow ourselves to be the example of this for others and ourselves.

Lesson 155
"I will step back and let Him lead the way."

What a wonderful invitation this lesson holds!

Give up thinking you are the one causing your good to come to you. Your good is already here. What we are instructed to do is to get out of the way. We were created in peace and love and joy and we remain there. Our only issue is that we think we must use our intellect to have this experience.

There is nothing to do; step away from the problem. Focus on God's gifts. These are ours by Divine Right, now. We are doing this not just for our own awakening, but also as an example to our brothers and sisters who are still lost in the illusion. Someone has to show the way.

We have been called and we have heard the call. Let us take the stand that we will let God lead the way. He knows where we are going. We walk to Him. Surely, He knows the way. As we practice letting go of the ego need to think that we are doing things on our own, our trust in the Love of God will become so natural that this life will become a peaceful journey Home.

Step back from all your worries and concerns and cares, and let God handle everything.

Lesson 156
"I walk with God in perfect holiness."

Accepting the Truth in this lesson, gives our life events greater importance.

We are the Bringers of Light to a dark and sad world. We are the Ones leading the way to the acceptance that we do not walk this earth alone, but that we all walk in holiness and joy with our Heavenly Father. No matter how often the ego guides us, that we walk this earth guilty and alone, we hold to this Truth.

In practicing the lessons set out for us by our darling brother, Jesus, the Truth of our Being becomes the only Identity we will allow. We are the holy expression of God. This is what we are. No matter what we have done or not done, we cannot change this. This idea is in the Mind of God and is eternal. Let us today, be vigilant in reminding ourselves that we walk with God in perfect holiness. PERFECT HOLINESS.

*"God's blessing shines upon me from within my heart, where He abides. I need but turn to Him, and **every sorrow melts away**, as I accept His boundless Love for me."* (ACIM)[51]

---

[51] W-207.1.2&3

Lesson 157
"Into His Presence will I enter now."

Jesus is telling us that this is one of the holiest days we can experience here in the illusion.

It is a day that we will glimpse our True Identity in Christ. Let us spend today silencing our ego thoughts, as much as we can, so that we will be in a position to enter into the Presence of our Loving Father. *"Into His Presence will I enter now."* Let this be our mantra as often as possible today. We ask the Holy Spirit to remind us to do this.

We can enter into the silence for just a minute and still receive the full effect of our dedication to the Truth. This is a day we spend with our Creator. We will visit as often as possible as we use the words of the title of this lesson. The grace that will come to us today is beyond measure. We are His Beloved and He is ours. Let us pause today and rest in this Awareness.

Today, we are at ease in the knowledge that we are sustained by the Love of God.

Lesson 158
"Today I learn to give as I receive."

I would suggest you read what this lesson has to say about time. It is very simple, yet profound.

The lesson in our Course is unceasing in its message. Whatever it is that we think about anyone or anything, we give but to ourselves. This should be obvious to us since our thoughts seem to live in our own mind. If we are holding a grudge or judgment against someone else, it is our own mind that is out of alignment with our Heavenly Father.

The other person may be going their way rejoicing as we torture ourselves with images of a past that no longer exists. The subconscious mind does not know the difference between what is happening now and what is a memory. The body reacts in the same way as when the original error was made. So it is that this lesson is reminding us to see our brothers and sisters as the Holy Creation of God. As we do this, we remember that this is our Identity as well.

In such a case, know that you do not see the person or circumstance in the Now Moment, but are seeing your past projected forward. Thus, forgiveness is called for. As we give these error thoughts to the Holy Spirit to forgive and heal for us, we see our world through vision, which is seeing through the eyes of the Holy Spirit. This is what we give the world and this is what we receive.

It is well worth the practice that this entails. *As we go out into our lives from this moment on, let us give ourselves the gift of thinking and speaking only words of love and healing.*

Lesson 159
"I give the miracles I have received."

What a fabulous invitation this lesson offers. It asks us to simply go to the Holy Spirit with any request that will bring us the happiness we deserve.

We cannot fail to receive the gift since it belongs to us already. We need the Holy Spirit because we have forgotten what is ours by Divine Inheritance. Remembering Who we are brings a blessing to the world as well. Accepting our gifts is what keeps us in touch with our Heavenly Home. How else can we remember Who and What we are unless we have experiences which bring this to our awareness.

Let's go now to Holy Spirit's garden and receive the bouquet that reveals our Father's Love for us. By doing this we will become a wonderful example, of His Love, with which to remind the world.

We are God's Beloved Creation and all that the Father has is ours for the asking. Let's ask. As we live a happy and holy life, we become a wonderful example for others to follow. Believe and all will be given to us freely.

Lesson 160
"I am at home. Fear is the stranger here."

Let us, this day, take back our home in God. Let our mind be returned to being in a place of quietness and joy.

The only thing the ego can do to confuse us is to suggest that we are not as God created us. We were created whole and complete and filled with joy. This is our home. This is where our safety lies. The harsh voice of the ego cannot change this. Its only power is the power that we give to its suggestions.

Either fear is real or Love is real. When fear thoughts appear in our mind, let's think of them as strangers knocking at our door. Ignore the temptation to look at them and let them dwell in your mind a while. Once we have allowed these fear thoughts entrance, it becomes even more difficult *not* to be affected by them.

We are at home in God, and in God we remain eternally. And what can threaten God Himself? Fear is not real and therefore is swallowed up into God's Love.

God has not given us a spirit of fear, but of power and love and a sound mind.

Lesson 161
"Give me your blessing, holy Son of God."

How fearful the world is to us as we see each other as bodies. We know what bodies are capable of. Newspapers, television, movies, etc., remind us perpetually of the danger inherent in bodies. But the Holy Spirit will use our belief that we are bodies as it does all error thought. It uses it to turn us back to God. Since we see each other as bodies, let us be willing to have the Holy Spirit reveal to us what is beyond the body. The body is simply a reflection of God.

By withdrawing our attention from the mirage that we call each other and allowing ourselves to see through the eyes of Jesus and the Holy Spirit, our lives will become the experience of Eden once again. Who could be afraid of an angel? This is how we must practice seeing each other; as the Earth Angels we are.

There is nothing anyone can do here in the illusion that can change our True Identity. God set this in motion. What could ever change this?

*"When you are afraid, be still and know that God is real, and you are His beloved Son in whom He is **well pleased**."* (ACIM)[52]

Lesson 162
"I am as God created me."

This wonderful lesson is repeated several times in the Course. It is a declaration of the Truth. In its simplicity, is its power.

We are as GOD created us, not as we made ourselves. We are powerful spiritual beings guided by wisdom and love. Where can fear and guilt intrude upon our holy minds with this held firmly in our thoughts?

The world we see screams that we are something different. It invites us to see ourselves as fearful, guilty and vulnerable. It presents evidence to us on a daily basis. However, as we repeat the title of this lesson many times, we will develop a mind muscle for this knowingness. As we become stronger in this awareness, we will bring this to the world. What greater purpose can we have but this?

With these words resounding in my mind, I am at peace. I AM AS GOD CREATED ME.

Lesson 163
"There is no death. The Son of God is free."

Father, bless our eyes today that we may see the reflection of your love in everything.

---

[52] T-4.I.8.6

What a wonderful mantra for us to use today. Unless we see the reflection of the Love of God in everyone and everything, we believe in the insanity of death. God is Life, and the giver of Life alone. When we see the sufferings of others, and ourselves, we are rejecting this Truth.

Let us today remove the blocks to the awareness of Love's Gifts. God is Love, Joy, Peace, Wholeness, Beauty and Freedom, to name a few. When we think we see something else, we believe that an illusion of the Truth can be real.

Let's speak and think the language of Life. It seems that at times, we cannot control our thoughts, but we can always control what we say. Let us start here. We no longer speak death talk, which includes sickness, anger, fear, envy etc. We allow the Holy Spirit to be the words in our mouth and the words in our ears.

We dedicate ourselves to knowing the Truth of our Being, which is Life, beautiful loving Life.

Lesson 164
"Now are we one with Him Who is our Source."

Oh, what a love letter this is from our brother, Jesus!

What a different world this would be if this were the story we heard from birth, instead of the scary fairy tales that were told to us and with which we still scare ourselves. Right now we can make the decision to exchange the senseless messages of this tired old world for the ever new and wonderful words of Truth.

In the words of this lesson, let us now "exchange all suffering for joy this very day". We can do this by being in the Now Moment and letting go all future fear and past regrets. By doing this, the Love of God will be revealed to our mind, and all good things will be added unto us. The Voice for God is always speaking to our minds. We can only hear It in the Silence. The senseless musing of a frighten mind must be quieted.

The Mighty Voice of Truth will be revealed, and we will know that we are Home.

Lesson 165
"Let not my mind deny the Thought of God."

The Lovingness of God is so evident in this lesson.

It is instructing us to ask for what we truly want. Yet, Jesus understands that we are not sure that we want the *Thought of God* in place of our meaningless desires. The Course gently leads us to the Truth by asking us to take baby steps. We are told to ask for the Thought of God, even if we are not sure this is the only thing we want.

When we are experiencing something in our lives that is not peaceful, it seems unnatural to give up our desire for the form, and to surrender to the peace that we really desire. Practice thinking, I desire_____ (name yours) then say, what I really want is the Peace of God. We will come to realize that this *is* our only desire and to experience this Peace.

The illusions we have used to mask the Peace of God have no real meaning for us. We want the Thought of God which created us, and is with us always. This is our heart's desire. By apprehending that this is Who and What we are eternally, the joy that is our strength, takes us through the illusion without suffering any of the effects of its falsity.

We are God's Beloved and God is our Beloved. We think the Thoughts of our Beloved and we are protected and provided for always. And this is how it is intended.

Lesson 166
"I am entrusted with the gifts of God."

The whole lesson is such a wonderful reminder that God is the only Authority in our lives.

This lesson reminds us repeatedly that God's Will reigns

supreme. All other thoughts, words and deeds are just false imaginings with which we frighten our minds. God created us to be happy and powerful. We either accept this as our Truth, or we allow something we made up to be the truth of our being.

How foolish to have this even be an issue. There is no doubt that everyone wants the contentment that the Love of God bestows upon us. This is the Will of God, and what God wills for us is so. As we live from this perspective, our lives become Heaven on earth and in so doing, we become examples of the Love of God. This gift is bestowed upon all who are willing to be aware of this Truth. Let us go out into our lives and live life as an example of the Love and Peace of God. Let us be the ones whose lives reflect the Goodness and Love of God in all forms. What could draw more people to seek God than awareness of the fruits of the Grace of God?

Father, Your Will and only your Will is the Truth in our lives. And so it is.

Lesson 167
"There is one life, and that I share with God."

And so the question "What am I?"$_{(ACIM)}$[53] *arises once again.*

Am I a body or am I Spirit? If I am a body, there is no doubt that the thing I call life is not one with the Father. This thing the world calls life can be snuffed out in a moment. If we are Spirit, the Life Force that emanates from the Father goes on in another form. It goes on in the realm of the Invisible. Nothing changes but the form. But it is to this form that the world bows.

How many of us have had a sure communion with our loved ones who have put on invisibility? I know I have many times. The only problem one has, or I should say I have, is that the ego voice tells me I am making it up. I have had too many experiences to be fooled by this any longer. There is one life and it goes on eternally.

---

[53] Part II.14

The opposite of Death is not Life. The opposite of Death is Birth. We did not begin at birth and we do not end at death. We go on in our consciousness as we always have. What God created as Life remains as Life, no matter what foolishness we make up to the contrary. There is one life and that is God. Since I am One with God, I am that Life also.

Thankfully, the Truth is true. And nothing we can do can change this. Amen

Lesson 168
"Your grace is given me. I claim it now."

This is another wonderful lesson that is leading us to the awareness of the Love that we are.

The Course uses the word 'grace' to mean our natural state. It also uses it to mean gift. God's Gift is His Love. No matter what we have done or not done, we are entitled to His Loving Kindness and all that it entails. There is nothing we need to do to convince God to forgive and love us. This is given. The problem lies in our love and forgiveness of ourselves.

When we surrender to God's View of us, all the gifts of the Kingdom become evident to us. It is God's Love that is our Heart's desire, nothing else. Once we experience the Love of God for us, all else fades.

Let us join in making this a day where we remind ourselves unceasingly that God's Love is ours right now.

As we relax into this Truth, the Love of God will overtake us, and we will be where we were meant to be, safe in the arms of our Creator.

Lesson 169
"By grace I live. By grace I am released."

This lesson extends a wonderful invitation to us.

It invites us to once again return to the Father's House and enjoy the benefits of being the beloved Child of God. It asks us to simply remember Who we are and What belongs to us. We need but take the tiny step of being willing to allow the Holy Spirit to heal our minds of the foolishness with which we have cluttered it and allow the Light of God to shine once more.

We are entitled to all that the Father has. It is through grace that this is our inheritance. There is nothing we can do to earn God's Loving gifts.

Our part is to surrender the need to refuse the gifts and open our minds and hearts to the Love and Blessings that are ours eternally.

Lesson 170
"There is no cruelty in God and none in me."

What a relief to know that God created us and we did not create God!

The God that we seemed to have created is such a fearful figure. It is the God of the Old Testament that most of us deep down in our hearts sometimes still believe exists. If you think this is not the case with you, just watch your thoughts when things are going badly in your life. If you are like me, you may temporarily slip back to the old way of begging God to relent and let us be relieved of the punishment we are experiencing for our past *sins*.

When we are in a good place, of course, this is absolutely ridiculous. But, there are still remnants of the old lessons we have been taught as children. That god is a punishing god, a god who has favorites and a god that demands sacrifices. How absolutely wonderful it is that we have been wrong, so very wrong. There is no such cruelty in God, and since we are created in the image and likeness of God, there is actually no cruelty in any of us.

It is true that we hear of cruel things happening in the world, but no longer can we ascribe these to God. These occurrences are examples of the belief in separation from God. As we awaken to our Identity, the only experience we can have of God is Great Love. It was not God that seemed to have chased us out of His Garden of Eden, but error thought about ourselves and about God.

How wonderful it is to know that we remain images of our Creator, loving, kind and powerful. Amen.

Lesson 171
"Review of Lessons 151 & 152."

"God is but Love, and therefore so am I."

This is the only thought we need hold to keep us in the Peace and Love and Joy of our true Identity. This is the echo of the Voice for God that calls us Home. This is the decision we must make. Are we as God created us, and constantly reminds us, or not? Or are we fearful, lonely souls adrift on the sea of an illusion that makes no sense? It is up to us to choose which to experience. It is not up to us to choose What we are, but through the gift of free will, we can choose to be One with God's Voice or separate and alone.

*Let us choose **Love** this day, and live in Love from now on. Let us live so as to remind one another that Love is real and nothing else really exists.*

Lesson 172
"Review of Lessons 153 & 154."

If we were to accept the fact that we were created in Love and in Love we remain, fear would be a meaningless concept.

In fact, fear would no longer exist in our consciousness. As fear is dissolved, what would One who lives and moves and has Its Being in God need to defend against? We are always being brought back to the remembering of the Truth about ourselves. We are as GOD created us, not what we made of ourselves. In this knowing, how easy it becomes to be among the ministers of God. Our lives become the examples of what accepting our True Identity looks like.

We are the Love of God. All good and only good is ours now and forever more.

Lesson 173
"Review of Lessons 155 & 156."

These lessons contain such a wonderful reminder that we are the Love of God in expression.

Jesus repeats this three times in each lesson. How wonderful it will be when we truly accept that we are BUT Love, nothing but Love. The Love of God in expression, limitless in power and in peace.

Where the Review of Lesson 155 states, "*I will step back and let Him lead the way,*" it is giving us a way of living the life of Love which we are. Inasmuch as we allow ourselves to flow with the Will of God, life becomes the happy dream it was meant to be. All struggle and strain fade away into nothingness.

We step back and allow ourselves to walk with God in our natural state, which is perfect holiness. There is no guilt in God and there is no guilt in us. Guilt is simply the suggestion of the ego, which is the part of our mind that is least in touch with Who we truly are. But, with this review, we are reminded that guilt is just a false judgment of Who we are. We walk with God in PERFECT HOLINESS. Perfect holiness does not include fear and guilt.

When we accept our **True Identity** *we become the Light of the World, which is intended in our Creation.*

Lesson 174
"Review of Lessons 157 & 158."

Into the Presence of Love do we enter, now.

We have been invited, and we accept, the invitation of returning to the remembrance of the Presence of God. What could be a more valuable experience! God's Presence, the Presence of eternal love and peace and joy, is awaiting our return. Let this be the day that we accept. Together, *now*, let us enter into the Presence of our Almighty Father and join with each other in the Great Awakening. This is the time. *Now* is the only real time there is. *Now* is the closest we can get to eternity here in the illusion of time. We let go all our doubts now, and relax into the Eternal Timelessness of Now.

What peace awaits this simple decision. Now, now, now, now. We're home.

Lesson 175
"Review of Lessons 159 & 160."

If we were to restate the affirmation repeated in these lessons it might bring that shift in perception to the Truth that we say we so desire.

I am BUT Love. I am nothing but the Light of God, the core of which is Living Love. Where Love is, there can be no fear. Thinking of Love as Light, we know that darkness cannot hold up against light, even the tiny light of a candle can bring light to a darkened room.

Thus as we live our lives, let us remember that even the simplest act of love can bring us huge results in relationships. Let's try to be aware of the times when love is called for. Since we answer this call, let us also observe its result. Nothing will be more convincing regarding the power of love than observing our own experiences.

Next time something tempts us to be fearful, let's shift our minds to extending love. We can simply think the word love again and again and again see what happens. I have done this often in my life and the results have been extraordinary. In fact, it has become natural for me to do so. *The Principles of Miracles* in the Text point out that when this does not occur, something has gone wrong. One will know this right away by the negative emotions one feels.

In every situation, love is what is called for. I am BUT Love, and so is everyone and everything. How simple is salvation!

Lesson 176
"Review of Lessons 161 & 162."

This lesson suggests we are to live our lives seeing one another as Love, as nothing but love.

This is the blessing we ask from each other and give to each other. What more could one ask than to be recognized as the Creation of Love. By virtue of holding in our heart and soul the Truth of our Being that we are as God created us, we demonstrate to our world that God/We are nothing but Love. What God created is eternal, and nothing can be added or taken away.

Guilt and fear have lost their seeming power and we live our lives, rejoicing in the endless love of God.

Lesson 177
"Review of Lessons 163 & 164."

The statement "God is but Love, and therefore so am I" brings us the gift of understanding of ourselves and the events of our lives, from the point of Love and not from fear.

When we interact with our sisters and brothers in this illusion, there is an inclination to perceive others as threats to our peace and joy. It seems that there is a limited amount of this energy and we must protect and defend what we have. But, when we realize that we *are* Love, created by Love, and in Love we remain, we know there is nothing to fear. Death becomes meaningless and we begin to live our lives as powerful spiritual beings, always and ever, One with our Creator.

Let's keep in mind that Love came first and filled all space. Nothing can change this. All we can do is pretend to be unaware of Love's Presence, which is always there behind all the foolish images we have made to hide Its presence.

Throughout the day let us frequently repeat the following statement: *God is but love, and therefore I am but love.* Continue doing this until it becomes our natural response to all that appears to happen during our time here in the body.

Our time here on earth will become the healing event it was meant to be. God is but love, and therefore I am but love.

Lesson 178
"Review of Lessons 165 & 166."

We are entrusted with the gifts of God, and in this trust is the awesome responsibility to be the Light that reveals those gifts to the world of illusion.

When we live from the awareness that God is nothing but Love, and so am I and everyone, the fear of each other that we often feel must dissolve. The gifts of God belong to everyone. There is no order of difficulty in miracles. The gifts of God were extended to us at our Creation and can never be changed in any way. This is the thought that must not be denied. We are His Beloved, now and forever more. And as His Beloved, peace, love, joy, freedom, wholeness, abundance, and beauty (to name a few of the gifts) are ours to enjoy and express.

There is no time like the Present. Let's return to the Garden and play.

Lesson 179
"Review of Lessons 167 & 168"

"There is but one life, and that I share with God.

If we were to accept this statement as the Truth about ourselves, sickness, sadness, or discomfort of any kind would be impossible. The Life and Love of God is that which appears as the heavens and earth. However, because of the ego guidance, we think there is such a thing as life **and** death. If God/Life is what is filling all space, where would death, illness, sadness, etc., reside? It could only reside in the imagination of the frightened mind.

We can easily let go all guilt and fear if we were to accept the grace of God right now. God's grace is our natural state. It is the gift of the Creator to the Created. Let us surrender our hold on whatever is blocking our awareness of the Life and Love of God. *God is but love, and therefore so am I,* now and forever more. Let us learn to speak only the language of Love and Life. As this becomes natural to us, we will experience only the Love and Life and Grace of God.

Thus, at last we awaken from the dream of separation, and be glad.

Lesson 180
"Review of Lessons 169 & 170."

Let's remember that Jesus repeated the line, "God is but love, and therefore so am I," three times in each review lesson.

This is the main teaching of the "A Course in Miracles." The Introduction to the Text states, *"the opposite of love is fear, but what is all-encompassing can have no opposite."* (ACIM)[54] Let us step forward into our lives from this day forward and remember that all that exists is love, or a call for love. Anything that seems to be negative is simply a call for the love that one does not think they deserve.

When we train our minds to come from love, no matter what appears in the outer, we will be well on our way to the Great Awakening. Jesus is asking us to be his voice, his eyes, his feet, and his hands through which we allow the Love of God to become evident on earth.

We are asked to take each other's hand and walk with him to Our Father's House. "It is Here that we find rest." (ACIM)[55]

---

[54] Introduction to A Course In Miracles
[55] Review V Introduction.12.6

The Lessons Illuminated
Lessons & Review of ACIM 181-220

WE ARE CERTAIN
we are protected and provided for in all our ways.
What could be more peaceful than this?

Illustrated by Cathleen Schott

Lesson 181
"I trust my brothers, who are one with me."

Let us not forget the message that Jesus gave to us in the Review we just completed.

God is but Love, and therefore so am I. When this becomes the truth of our being, the only thing we will see as we look out into the illusion is Love. Who does not trust those we love? When we forget that we are Love, fear becomes the only alternative and trust becomes impossible. If trust is absent, control and defense become the other choices.

There is a saying from the Course that I like to use that goes along with this lesson. It is: "*Everyone and everything I see will lean toward me to bless me. I will recognize in everyone my dearest Friend.*"$_{(ACIM)}$[56] And so our journey becomes one of trust and joy. The *dearest Friend* that we trust in everyone is the Holy Spirit.

This lesson is not asking us to be doormats for each other. We ask for guidance on how to handle all relationships. It is reminding us of Who we truly are and Who our brother truly is. From this vantage point, we trust that a part of our brother is coming from a higher place. Thus we recall that this is Who we truly are as well.

As we hold this place for one another and ourselves, it becomes easier for all to remember Who we are. Love, Love, Love, that is all there really is.

---

[56] W-60.3.4&5

Lesson 182
"I will be still an instant and go home."

"You have not lost your innocence. It is for this you yearn. This is your heart's desire."

I love this thought from today's lesson. There is such quietness and peace in this idea. This is the home for which we search. No matter how often we change people or houses or things in the outer world, we will not find what it is we truly desire.

We yearn to experience our Original State, which is one of innocence. If only we had been taught from childhood to help each other experience this innocence, what a different world this would be!

Instead, the ego has instructed us that to feel better about ourselves is to make others feel guilty. Thus we wander this world looking for our homes when we are at Home with God all along. Let us go into the silence and allow the Holy Spirit to reveal to us our true home. It is in innocence that we feel the safety and love, which we call *home*. As we become aware of this, we will extend it to others.

I am sure you have noticed that there are some people with whom you feel comfortable and peaceful. These are the ones who have uncovered their own innocence and are not extending guilt to others in order to feel some relief.

Let's go out into our world today, and in stillness see the innocence in others. Thus we will be reminded of our true home, which is the consciousness of innocence and love in which we were created.

Lesson 183
"I call upon God's Name and on my own."

While meditating on the name of God I deeply realized that this is my name as well.

I experienced a deep sense of contentment and joy. I felt as the prodigal son in the Bible must have felt as his father ran out to meet him. I realized that God is our only desire. God is the home we are seeking. God is present with us all the time, in all places and circumstances. What else is there to desire? The Father and I are One and in this Oneness is All there is.

I am having a difficult time typing this message this morning after having the deep realization of the Presence of God and My Self.

I must share with you something endearing. While sitting on my sofa, meditating on the name of God and my Self, my psychic cat Sandy jumped up on my lap and kept nudging the Course book and then laid down next to me. I realized he was telling me that he knew he was God appearing as cat. It was so touching. Once I realized what he was sharing with me, he walked away and lay down by my feet. This really gave me an even deeper experience that God is all there is.

God, God, God, your beloved returns.

Lesson 184
"The Name of God is my inheritance."

What can I add to the beautiful words in this lesson? All I can suggest is that we begin to train our minds to mentally call each person by his rightful name, which is God.

I know this is not feasible in the outer world, but if we were to think of each person as God-Mary, God-John, God-Irene, God-George, our mind will begin to be trained to see the Truth in all of us. Our name is God. By doing this we will begin to heal our sense of separation and differences. As this becomes more and more natural to us, the gifts of God will become manifest and we will truly experience Heaven on earth.

Lesson 185
"I want the peace of God."

I feel there is little I can add to the beautiful words that Jesus shares with us in this practice.

I guess the only thing I can suggest is that whenever you feel the desire for something of the illusion, remind yourself that what you really want is the peace of God. This is the goal of all goals. It is our natural state, and the goal of all our searching here. How strange that we search and search for something that belongs to us already.

"No one who truly seeks the peace of God can fail to find it. For he merely asks that he deceive himself no longer by denying to himself what is God's Will." (ACIM)[57]

Lesson 186
"Salvation of the world depends on me."

If you have the time and willingness, please read this whole lesson. There is so much in it on false humility, which I think we all need to hear.

The salvation of the world depends on our willingness to hear the Voice for God, the Holy Spirit, and carry out what we are guided to do. There is no mystery in this. The only function we have here on earth is to heal our mind. And as we heal our own error thoughts, the world is blessed.

Nothing is more valuable here on earth than to remove the blocks to the awareness of Love's presence in others and ourselves. As we see each other as the Christ, the world will bow to Its True Identity, and Love will prevail once more. What could be more important than this!!!

"Forgiveness is an earthly form of love which as it is in Heaven has no form. Salvation of the world depends on you who can

---

[57] W-185.11.1&2

forgive. Such is your function here."(ACIM)[58]

Let us today free ourselves from error thought by inviting the Holy Spirit into any thought that is not of the Light. In this way, our minds will Light the way for others, as those before us have done for us.

Lesson 187
"I bless the world because I bless myself."

This lesson contains a very important message for all of us.

One of the ego's favorite lies is the belief in scarcity and lack. It is from this belief that most of the world's problems emanate. If there is only a finite amount of good and love, then we must attack and defend and go to war for it. However, this is coming from level confusion.

When we think the form is what is to be possessed, we will definitely experience the fear of loss. However, when we realize that consciousness is the source of all that is seen and unseen, we will realize that as we give away what is in our consciousness, there can only be increase. I know that when I come to realize, at a deeper level, one of the Truths shared in our Course, then this Truth becomes more real for me.

When you give from a consciousness of love and gratitude and plenty, then this is what returns to you multiplied in the form you most need. It is only ideas that can be shared. And we are always sharing ideas of the ego or of the spirit. If we give from ego, we but make a bargain. I give to you, now you give to me. What a limited way of thinking. However, if we give from Spirit, we are giving from a sense of Oneness with God and each other. The return is unlimited because God is unlimited. No one loses and everyone gains.

You cannot out-give God. This is the way of the Kingdom and it is good; very, very good.

---

[58] W-186.14.2&5

Lesson 188
"The peace of God is shining in me now."

Oh my goodness, what a beautiful lesson this is! It reminds us of our true Identity as Light.

We are the Light of peace and darkness has no power over us. It is the Peace of God that shines from us and shows us Heaven on earth.

When we are not in the peace of God, we see shadow figures, which frighten us. We give names to these figures and then believe them real. But once we allow the Peace of God to shine in us, these figures disappear into the nothingness from which they came. In peace, there is nothing that can frighten us or harm us. We are the Light of the world because the Peace of God is shining in us now and as it blesses us, the world is blessed as well.

We want peace on earth, and the way to experience this is to know our Innocence. As we recognize our innocence, we are in line with the Thoughts of God.

Thus, we are certain that we are protected and provided for in all ways. What could be more peaceful than to be sure of this?

Lesson 189
"I feel the Love of God within me now."

How wonderful to know that the Love of God is always within us.

Our only responsibility is removing the blocks to the awareness of love's presence. *How foolish we are to value our petty little judgments and worries, when we can be in the Presence of the Love of God.* In this Presence all cares disappear. Do you remember how it feels when you are experiencing love for someone or something? In this state of mind, all worries and problems seem to disappear. This is our natural state. It is in the state of Divine Love, where nothing can intrude and rob our joy. Let's be vigilant and notice when we are not experiencing the

Love of God. Choose then to immediately go into forgiveness. The Love is there. It is simply being blocked from our awareness by the ego's lies. The Love of God is with us now, and we feel safe.

How blissful... and how natural.

Lesson 190
"I choose the joy of God instead of pain."

The title of this lesson has a very important word in it, and that word is **choose***.*

We are always One with the Joy of God, but it is through our false perceptions of who we are that we experience pain. If we truly knew we were One with the Father, pain would be impossible.

Another false perception that we hold is that God is cruel. When we clear our mind of these lies of the ego, pain disappears. Let us now call to our Heavenly Father. As it said in yesterday's lesson, *"Father, we do not know the way to You. But we have called and You have answered us. We will not interfere. Salvation's ways are not our own, for they belong to You."*(ACIM)[59] We go into the silence, leaving behind all thoughts of problems with our body, our finances, our relationships or whatever area in life we may be deceived, and invite the Thoughts of God to come to us.

In doing this we will notice that problem areas begin to improve. It is only in our thoughts that we are not as God created us (which is whole and complete and full of joy and innocence) that causes us any pain at all. When the ego presents these thoughts to us, let's use the words from this lesson, *Peace to such foolishness!* I have used these words many times in my life. I have used them when ego thoughts threaten my own peace of mind, and also I have used them silently when I am in the presence of someone else who is under the spell of the ego. These words are very powerful.

---

[59] W-189.10.1-3

Anything but the Will of God is foolishness. God sees us as holy and wills only joy for us.

It is up to us to choose the thoughts that will line us up with God's Will for us. We do this moment to moment, leaving behind past regrets and future imaginings. In the Now Moment, we are still as holy and innocent and good as God created us. In this Now Moment we are as close to God as we can get in the illusion.

In this moment we are One with God. What else would we sanely choose but our True Identity in Christ?

Lesson 191
"I am the holy Son of God Himself."

"There is nothing my holiness cannot do because the power of God lies in it." (ACIM)[60]

What a statement! If we were only to accept the Truth that is shared with us constantly in so many forms and so many times, we would know ourselves as the powerful spiritual beings that we are. But somehow the ego lies seem more easily accepted. Our Course tells us the reason for this. *"Into eternity, where all is one there crept a tiny, mad idea, at which the Son of God remembered not to laugh."* (ACIM)[61] That idea is that we separated ourselves from the care of our Loving Creator. We choose to believe that we are orphans and must live life on our own. Peace to such foolishness. We are the holy Son of God, Himself. And so are we entitled to all the gifts of God.

Let us today once again take our rightful place in the Kingdom. We do this by giving up control and trusting God's Love and by relaxing into the Everlasting Arms of our Father. Thus, we release the need to think that we are alone and comfortless. Pain, sickness, and loss are but ideas unknown to God. We return to our Father's House, with a sigh of relief that we were wrong. We are the holy Son of God, and we happily accept this today. We

---

[60] W-38.5.3
[61] T-27.VIII..6.2

are free now and we offer this freedom to the world we see.

Lesson 192
"I have a function God would have me fill."

There is little I can say about the benefits of forgiveness that has not been said before, over and over again.

However, I would like to suggest that we use our function of forgiveness to forgive ourselves. Whenever you feel yourself judging anything about your life, immediately give it to Spirit to forgive and heal for you. The clues that forgiveness of ourselves is called for is when we notice that we are thinking: I should, I should not have, I wish I had not, or whatever is your particular way of telling yourself that you did it wrong, or that you are not enough.

We all have our own personal ways of judging ourselves. Let's become more and more aware of these times and let them go, so that the joy and love that is our natural inheritance can be experienced once more. Forgive yourself. It all is as it is meant to be.

As we flow with life, not resisting, we will find ourselves back in the comfort of our Father's Arms. And this is how it is intended.

Lesson 193
"All things are lessons God would have me learn."

The only lesson that God would have us learn, no matter what the form it may take, is that if we are not in peace, we are in error.

Error calls for forgiveness, not blame. We are being reminded that God's Will for us is perfect happiness and it is only the thoughts accepted from the ego that blocks our experience of this. We will forgive, and we will see this differently. This statement shows that God's Joy is always with us, waiting but our acceptance.

Forgiveness can be thought of as simply removing any judgments we hold against others or ourselves. As these error thoughts are erased, the Thoughts of God become evident. In the Now Moment, we are returned to the awareness of Love's Presence, and we relax in the peace and safety of our rightful place in God's plan. Thus, whenever we are aware that we are out of peace, instead of looking for reasons and who to blame, we bring our mind to forgiveness and the Light returns to our mind once more. It is really this simple. *Profound, but simple.*

Lesson 194
"I place the future in the hands of God."

Before we begin, I would like to share with you that this lesson and lessons 48 & 50 are my emergency lessons. Some people call 911, I call 48, 50 & 194.

When we are wading through troubled waters, it often seems difficult to place the future in the Hands of God. When we realize that all we are being asked is to do is be in the *Now Moment*, then it seems more doable.

The past and future do not exist in the Kingdom, and so they are not real. We are being asked to place our belief in nothingness in the Hands of God and trust in the Present. Surely, we can trust minute to minute. It is when the ego mind takes us into the fearful future that we get lost. God is in charge of eternity and eternity exists only in the Now Moment. Therefore, there is nothing to fear. Our future is assured, as it becomes an extension of a joyful present. We rest, now knowing only good can come.

An effective visual for me when I am concerned about someone or something, is to envision huge beautiful hands extending out from the sky and then to place my concerns into them.

This gives me the feeling of letting go, allowing the Love of God to do Its perfect work.

Lesson 195
"Love is the way I walk in gratitude."

As with all attributes of God, the ego makes counterfeit of gratitude.

The ego knows gratitude is inherent in Love, so it takes this emotion, turns it around, and invites us to think we are grateful to God when we are thankful that our lives are not as bad as someone else's. How foolish we have been to believe this idea.

The only true gratitude is the gratitude that emanates from love and not from fear. I am sure you have noticed how appreciated you felt when you gave someone a gift and they remarked on how much they LOVE the gift. As they express their feelings and say, *"Oh I love this"*, we feel such happiness that they have received the love that inspired it. This is how it is with the Love of God. As we are conscious of the gratitude we feel because we are One with God and each other, we walk the way of Love.

Consequently, we walk the way to God.

Lesson 196
"It can be but myself I crucify."

How often do we need to be reminded that our thoughts are the determiner of our experiences?

Our beloved Jesus proved this to us on the cross. Even while being physically crucified in the outer, he did not crucify himself by judging those who were doing this to him. He showed us how to keep our mind on the Holy Spirit no matter what is occurring in our lives. He asks us in the text; can you not do this in less extreme circumstances? We seem to answer that no, we cannot. But he has showed us what is possible and we are asked to have a little willingness to discipline our minds in order to accomplish this same thing. He said you are not asked to be literally crucified, but just to know the power of your thoughts.

No one is pushing our buttons. We installed the buttons and we push them when things do not occur as we expect or demand.

Let's stop this foolishness. We are of God. There is nothing outside us that can hurt or injure us unless we give it the power to do so. From this day forward, let us allow ourselves to know Who we are and Who God is.

"God did not give us a spirit of fear, but of power and love and a sound mind." [62] *Let us accept this gift of God now.*

Lesson 197
"It can be but my gratitude I earn."

Let's remember the Course is always referring to mind, and not to anything in the outer.

So the gift that we are giving and seemingly taking back is Love. It is not the outer action that has any significance, but it is the love that inspires it. How often have we felt offended if someone does not seem to show appreciation for what we have done for them or given them. We are tempted by the ego to become angry or hurt and withdraw the love that inspired the gift.

As we know, what we do to others we will think can be done to us. The more we think we can withdraw the love we offer another (in any form), the more we will believe that God will abandoned us if we do not live up to the standard WE set for God. And so, dear friends on the Path, let's remember that all that we give, we give unto God.

God has great gratitude, to us, for remaining the lovers that He created us to be. Therefore, let us offer each other only the Love of God with no strings attached. As we go about our lives, let us be kind to one another. It is not so much what we do for each other, but how we do it. Let's come from compassion and love. As we do this we will know that all is done for God and returned to us multiplied.

We cannot out give the Love of God.

---

[62] 2 Timothy 1:7 New King James Version (NKJV)

Lesson 198
"Only my condemnation injures me.

How simple is the solution to all the world's problems, as well as our own. We simply need to remember that all that we give we give to ourselves.

We actually believe that by holding judgmental thoughts against the world, we will find peace. The only way this would make *sense* is to believe the ego's suggestions of our own guilt. Those who remember their own holiness and innocence find that judgment and condemnation has more or less disappeared from their mind. When we judge or condemn we are trying to project the guilt we feel within ourselves onto others. The ego says this is the way to freedom from the pain of forgetting that we are as God created us.

Forgiveness leads us back to the remembrance of our true Identity. We are holy. We were created holy and this is how we remain.

As we allow forgiveness to do its mighty work in our mind, this will become more and more evident that it is the Truth about everyone and us.

Remember, the Course says that the only thing that stands between the Father and the Son is guilt. When we allow forgiveness to remove this guilt, the separation will be no more, and Heaven will again be our only experience. Thy Will be done on earth as it is in Heaven.

God's Will is for us to experience perfect happiness now, today.

Lesson 199
"I am not a body. I am free."

It is clear from the message of this lesson that we think we are a body when we are depending on the ego for guidance.

We think we are separate and alone, as the body appears to be. The ego has kept this thought available to all on earth in so many ways. The body is thought to be either the source of joy or of pain. But the valuing of the body has never brought us what we really want, which is the peace and love of God. The ego says it will, but we surely know by now that this is not true.

The body may bring temporary pleasure or temporary relief, but it is very fleeting. Soon there is something else to want or to heal. Thus, the only way to free ourselves of the body is to listen only to the guidance of the Holy Spirit. This is the Voice that speaks for God and for our True Identity. It is our Real Self held in trust while we dilly-dally with the ego. Please reread the last sentences quoted above and accept the absolute Truth of this statement. And thus, the world will come to know its True Self once more and Peace will reign on the planet.

Let's imagine this until we see it come to pass.

Lesson 200
"There is no peace except the peace of God."

How easy this lesson makes it sound to have the peace of God. However, as we know, when we are in the middle of an ego attack, it does not seem to be easy. The illusion appears to be quite real.

The steps that have worked for me in these cases are JESUS:
Join with another like (Love/Light) minded person.
Ego voice always lies.
Stay in the Now Moment, no matter what is going on.
Use the forgiveness prayer. (cited below)
Surrender the outcome.

While we practice one or all of these steps, keep in mind that what we truly want is the peace of God and nothing else will satisfy. As the Holy Spirit takes over we realize that if God did not create the situation, it is not real. When we say *real* we mean, not eternal. Remind yourself that this is temporary. This disarms the ego's whisperings that *this will never end.*

Let us join today in practicing the statement suggested in this lesson: *"There is no peace except the peace of God, And I am glad and thankful it is so."*

Forgiveness Prayer:
Holy Spirit, whatever this represents, I give it to you to forgive and heal for me. Take this from me and heal it for me. Don't let me use this to hurt myself anymore. Behind this is a miracle to which I am entitled. And I joyously receive my miracle now. Thank you. Amen

Lesson 201
"Review of Lesson 181."

So, we come to our next review. As with the previous review, there is a central thought that is repeated with each lesson.

As we practice with the thought offered us by Jesus, we will come to know our Self as we were created. And knowing Who we are, so will we know Who our brother truly is. Thus, we will live our lives in a friendly world, where we recognize everyone as family. No matter what seems to be the appearance being presented to us, we will see behind the mask and recognize the Christ in each other. As this becomes our experience, we will naturally trust our brothers, who are one with us.

One more thought, if you read the introduction to this series of lessons you will find a wonderful recommendation from Jesus. He suggests that when tempted by an ego thought we say, *"This thought I do not want. I choose instead _____."*

I think this is an excellent opportunity for us to become aware of our thoughts and choose the thoughts of Holy Spirit instead of unconsciously thinking from the ego. Let's practice this together.

Lesson 202
"Review of Lesson 182."

"I will be still an instant and go home." This lesson asks us to still the senseless musings of the ego mind and allow ourselves to return to the Now Moment where we are at home.

It asks, *"Why would I choose to stay an instant more where I do not belong?"* Somehow, we feel more *at home* in our thoughts about the past, future, analyzing and planning than in surrendering to the Holy Spirit's gentle messages.

Through *practice* we are beginning to realize, step by step, that our only goal is the peace of God. To experience this we must give up the *cheap thrill* of scaring ourselves with thoughts that mean nothing. We are at Home in the Arms of God and it is here we remain, no matter how the ego tempts us to think otherwise. *"To be in the Kingdom is merely to focus your full attention on it."* (ACIM)[63]

There is no other Home that will satisfy us. And so, we give up looking for it anywhere but in the Now Moment.

Lesson 203
"Review of Lesson 183."

Our review lessons are guiding us to freedom. And how can we be free, if we do not know our Identity.

Only true freedom is found by not accepting the ego's suggestions of Who we are. Our Name is Christ, Our Name is Freedom, Our name is Love, Our Name is Joy, Our Name is any and all the attributes of God. We seem to have a body's name but this name is so limiting. We are so much more. When in one of the ego attacks that the ego is so good at offering to us, let us remember Who we are. We are heirs of God.

This is our Name, and in this name abides our freedom and joy.

Lesson 204
"Review of Lesson 184."

Our inheritance gives us our Identity as a Spiritual Being guided

---

[63] T-III.4.1

by Wisdom and Love. This is our *name*. We have called ourselves by many names, all of which have limited us. We are free when we know ourselves as heirs of God. Today, let us allow God to define Who we are. *It is good, very, very good.*

Lesson 205
"Review of Lesson 185."

Oh, how true this lesson is!

No matter how strong the desire to be peaceful is, the ego is frantic in its urging us to want to be right. But *right* has never brought us what we truly desire. We want the peace of God so that the memory of God can return to our awareness. "*The memory of God comes to the quiet mind.*"$_{(ACIM)}$[64]

In our need to be right, the mind is never satisfied. If you are willing, think of whatever is troubling us today and decide that what we really want is the peace of God, and nothing else. If it seems difficult to do this, then practice staying in the present moment.

Our Course assures us that peace will come flooding into our holy minds.

Lesson 206
"Review of Lesson 186."

The salvation of the world depends on the healing of our mind and the removal of the blocks to Love's Presence.

Love is the core of the gifts of God to which we are entrusted, and to which we are asked to share with those who people our world. If each of us heals our own mind, the ego would be no more.

We are sent those who are to benefit from our spiritual work, just as we are being sent to those who help us on our spiritual path. We are here to remind each other that we are not bodies. We are

---

[64] T-23.I.1.1

Spirit and holy Children of God.

In this knowing, peace will reign once more as it did in the Garden. And this is how it is intended.

Lesson 207
"Review of Lesson 187."

"Every sorrow melts away, as I accept His boundless Love for me." What a wonderful line to contemplate.

"Every sorrow" is but the turning away from the Love that we are. *"God, being Love, is also happiness."* (ACIM)[65] If each of us would be willing to accept the Love of God, the world would be blessed indeed. But somehow the ego has convinced us that to judge others and ourselves is the way to peace. What a faulty premise this is.

Let's think about a time when we felt great love for someone or something, and remember the peace that we experienced. It is only the thought now I can't love you" that leads us to judgment and pain. How foolish we have been!! Only God's Love is real. Everything else is error thought. Let's begin to live our lives now based on what is real. In this way, we will be a blessing to the world and ourselves.

I leave you with the words from this lesson; "Every sorrow melts away, as I accept His boundless Love for me."

Lesson 208
"Review of Lesson 188."

To know that we are still as God created us is the answer to all the ego's senseless thoughts.

In peace we were created, in peace we remain. However, we can

---

[65] W-L.103

remain in the Heart of our Peaceful and Ever loving God and still allow our mind to wander away from this. Of course, we cannot do this in truth, but we do this in our imagination. Thus, as this lesson suggests, it is when we still our minds and listen for the Voice for God that we remember that we are still as peaceful as God created us.

In the stillness of our mind and heart does God become evident to us. Be still and know that I am God. And we are Home once more.

Lesson 209
"Review of Lesson 189."

What freedom there is to feel the Love of God within us. You probably have read or heard the old question: **What would you do if you were not afraid?** *Well, this lesson asks us to surrender to the Love of God and to trust It.*

The Love of God is the goal of all our seeking here. It is the only thing we truly desire because it is our natural state. Fear has no power over us when we feel This Love. Even in the illusionary world, we probably have all experienced this. When we are *in love* or loving a baby or an animal or a cause, notice how fear is not present. Remember, there are only two choices, love or fear. If we choose to think that fear is real, we lose the Kingdom of God and all its gifts. However, in choosing Love, all is restored to our awareness. Love or fear, choose which one we serve with our thinking today. Which will we magnify?

Let us magnify the Lord and return to our rightful place in the Kingdom of God.

Lesson 210
"Review of Lesson 190."

Pain is not His Will!

Let us be willing to accept this without reservations. Even the lessons that we think we are to learn here are not meant to be painful. The only pain we feel is caused by our own thinking. The thought that usually causes our pain is the resistance to what is.

Joy is the Will of God for us, and this is our will also. The problem does not lie with God, but with ourselves. No matter what occurs, if we were to think the Thoughts of God (I take ideas from the Course as the thoughts of God), we would notice that pain is lessened if not erased from our experience. Sure, we may have to repeat the thought many times until it *takes*, but so what. We are thinking anyway. Why not think the Thoughts of God, of Love and Joy?

God did not give us a spirit of fear, but of power and love and a sound mind,"[66] *and we accept only this now.*

Lesson 211
"Review of Lesson 191."

"In silence and in true humility," are the secrets to experiencing ourselves as God created us.

There is no way we can have this experience when the mind is frantic with ego thinking. Furthermore, there is no way we can do so, unless we are willing to let go of the false idea we have of who we are, and allow God's Idea to become our own.

Why would we want to hold on to the pitiful picture we have made of God's Son, when God's Power and Glory are available to us? We are as God created us. God created us as an Invisible Idea. We must go back to experiencing ourselves in essence. The body is the visibility and tangibility of this Idea. We are not the body. We have a body while in the illusion as a teaching device. It can be used by the Holy Spirit to teach Truth or the ego to foster its lies. We are as God created us whether we accept this or not.

Let's accept this and let God live our lives today.

---

[66] 2 Timothy 1:7 New King James Version (NKJV)

Lesson 212
"Review of Lesson 192."

Our function is to forgive and be happy. This is what our dear Course tells us unceasingly.

Joy was created for us, and to experience this true joy we must be in alignment with the Thoughts of God. There is no provision for thoughts that are judgmental. It is only when we allow the Holy Spirit to Light our mind once more with the Thoughts of God that we can experience ourselves as we were created to be. God created us in Its Image and Likeness. Any other image will only bring pain and suffering.

Let us allow today to be the day when we surrender to God's Idea of What we truly are. Healing our mind is the most important function we can have now or ever. We are the Joy Bringers to this tired old world. To do so, we must forgive our errors and the errors of other unawake souls. In this way, we become the highest example of Love for others to follow.

What could be more joyful than this?

Lesson 213
"Review of Lesson 193."

*In the course of going through our **little** episodes of healing, it surely does not feel that there is a miracle waiting for us. At this point in our learning, we can have faith that this truly is the case.*

Events occur that can seem to be very painful, but our Course assures us that this is a lesson that God would have me learn. And what we are to learn is that we are still as God created us. We cannot be hurt or injured except by our ego thoughts. We are being shown the blocks to the awareness of God's Presence in our Mind.

If we resist the removal of these ego beliefs, we suffer. However, if we re-frame them and allow ourselves to know that this is happening FOR us, not TO us, we will soon know the joy of release from yet another of the egos ploys to keep us from our peace and joy.

As it states in lesson 193, "*To all that speaks of terror, answer thus: I will forgive and this will disappear.*" "*And God would have all tears be wiped away, with none remaining yet unshed, and none but waiting their appointed time to fall.*"

"*For God has willed that laughter should replace each one, and that His Son be free again.*" (ACIM)[67]

Lesson 214
"Review of Lesson 194."

Isn't it amazing how difficult it sometimes seems to place the future in the Hands of God?

First of all, the future is illusionary, so we are really trusting God with nothing. Secondly, what we are actually doing is placing ourselves, in the present, in the Hands of Love. As we have been taught many a time in so many ways, God is Love, and that Love only gives. We know that when we turn things over to God everyone wins and no one loses. Surely, we have enough experience of this to trust.

As it suggests in Lesson 194, let's "*release the future*" so that we may live joyously and peacefully in the Now Moment.

Remember that no matter what is going to happen, God and you can handle it, with ease.

Lesson 215
"Review of Lesson 195."

The most grateful words one can say to another when receiving a gift are, "*I love it!*" The Holy Spirit is guiding us to see our world in this way. As we look on a beautiful scene or the beautiful face of a loved one, the feelings that come up are love

---

[67] W-193.9.5

and gratitude. This is the experience we aspire to as we let the Holy Spirit be our guide in all things.

As our Master Teacher Jesus said, the only true commandment is; *Love God and love your neighbor as yourself.* What a peaceful world this would be if we all disciplined our minds to think in this way.

The way to Heaven is a way of love and gratitude and where one is so must the other be found.

Lesson 216
"Review of Lesson 196."

This idea is repeated often in our Course. It is the central point of the lessons leading us to peace of mind.

The ego would have us believe that to attack another is the way to release ourselves from our own feelings of guilt. It hides from us that to think attack thoughts are to crucify ourselves with the guilt we feel. There is only one way to God, and that is through true forgiveness. True forgiveness is to withdraw all judgments and allow our mind to rest in the Thoughts of God. Attack thoughts are not true and have no power, but they do affect our bodies. This we all know for sure.

We are being taught to give up nothing, in exchange for everything. Therefore, forgiveness is the path to experiencing our Selves as we were created, which is whole and compete and full of joy.

Is it such a small price to pay for such a tremendous return?

Lesson 217
"Review of Lesson 197."

To have the experience that we are not the body and that we are free brings the elimination of any need for outside gratitude.

Focusing our attention on Creation brings all that the Father has into our awareness. In our Creation we were given everything, and the outer is a manifestation of the degree to which we have accepted this. Every gift is given to God, which is Who we are. Therefore, the real gratitude is to ourselves for being willing to turn our mind to the Thoughts of God and to experience the gifts that this brings forth.

As we seemingly give to others, we keep in mind that we are but instruments of God's Will for happiness for others and from them to ourselves. How joyful it is to know that we are channels of God's Love.

What more gratitude could we desire than to be grateful that we have this awareness!

Lesson 218
"Review of Lesson 198."

It is only through the erroneous use of grievances and judgments that we cannot see our own glory as God created us.

When we misuse the mind in this manner, we lose our way and begin to think from the ego's perception. Nothing can change the truth No matter what we do, think or say, we are still as God created us. We can hide our eyes to that fact, but it stands ready behind every ego thought.

The first step is to realize that we are listening to a voice that is not the Voice for God. The Holy Spirit's Voice will never guide us away from our remembrance of Who we are and Who we will always remain. What God created is eternal. It is only the time we take to remember who we are that is at our command. Let's allow that time be Now, today, this very moment. We ARE as God created us. We are all beautiful, free, holy, loving, peaceful and on and on.

Why wait?? Heaven is here now.

Lesson 219
"Review of Lesson 199."

Without end, our dear brother, Jesus, repeats the thought "I am not a body. I am free." This is the primary correction needed for the Great Awakening to occur.

We are Spirit, invisible, powerful, beloved Spirit. The body can be the outer picture of our true Identity. However, now it is the pictorial representation of our thoughts. When we allow the Holy Spirit to be our only guide, our physical body will reflect its true essence. It is a body of Light, the substance of which is Living Love.

As we train our mind to think from this vantage point, we will begin to experience Who we truly are. We may still not be perfect at doing this, but the intent is what is important. As we become more willing to release the need to magnify the original error thought (that we can be separate from the Love and Protection and Provision of our Creator) our body will reflect only the Wholeness and Joy that was intended in our Creation.

We are as God created us. Let us rejoice and be glad that this is so. Practice, Practice, Practice.

Lesson 220
"Review of Lesson 200."

*Only the Holy Spirit knows the **way of peace**, and surely we have experienced the Truth of this many, many times in our lives.*

We have tried to find other ways, judgment, blame, analyzing, equalizing etc., but we have never found what we really wanted. Oh, the ego will guide us to continue using our mind in this way, but the ego's goal is to be right. Being right has never brought us permanent peace. Ego gratification is sometimes instant, but not lasting. However, following the Holy Spirit's Divine guidance has led us to peace that endures.

Yes, there may be other lessons or other aspects of error thought, but once we have truly surrendered our judgments to the Holy Spirit, the awareness of God's Love and Peace returns.

We are Home at last Love.....Mary Barbara

The Lessons Illuminated
Part II, Lessons ACIM 221-365

We have come to Part II of the Workbook. This section guides us to the experience of quiet communication with our Father. It asks us to meditate on the words of the lesson and wait for an experience of the Presence of God.

Illustrated by Cathleen Schott

PART II - Introduction

"Instead of words we need but feel His Love."

The introduction to this section is just lovely. I would suggest you read it and hear it as a love letter from Jesus.

You might want to actually imagine that it begins with Dear _____(your name) and ends with, Love... Jesus. Before each series of lessons in Part II of the Workbook, there is a page that says "What is forgiveness", "What is Holy Spirit", etc. The following lessons were developed from these pages.

It is powerful to read daily the page that corresponds to the lessons.

I feel guided to take one thought from the lesson or the introduction or the "What is" section and suggest that we use it to contemplate during the day. I feel this guidance coming from the first several sentences at the beginning of Part II.

I will quote them now. "*Words will mean little now. We will use them but as guides on which we do not depend. For now we seek DIRECT EXPERIENCE of truth alone.*"

The following is our contemplation for today: "*Father, I come to you today to seek the peace that You alone can give.*"

Lesson 221 - "Peace to my mind. Let all my thoughts be still."
Suggested thought to contemplate: *"Father, I come to you today to seek the peace that You alone can give."*

Lesson 222 - "God is with me. I live and move in Him."
Suggested thought to contemplate: *"God is with me."* Let's allow this to be the answer to every trial we may perceive today, and also as a gentle happy reminder throughout the day.

Lesson 223 - "God is my life. I have no life but His." Suggested thought to contemplate: *"Now I know my life is God's."*

Lesson 224 - "God is my Father, and He loves His Son."
Suggested thought to contemplate: *"Father, reveal to me what you would have me see today."*

Lesson 225 - "God is my Father, and His Son loves Him."
Suggested thought to contemplate: *"The memory of God is shimmering across the wide horizons of our minds."*

Lesson 226 - "My home awaits me. I will hasten there."
Suggested thought to contemplate: *"Father, Your arms are open to me."*

Lesson 227 - "This is my holy instant of release." Suggested thought to contemplate: *"Father, I am so close to you, I cannot fail."*

Lesson 228-"God has condemned me not. No more do I." Suggested thought to contemplate: *"And now we wait in silence, unafraid and certain of God's coming."*

Lesson 229 - "Love, Which created me, is what I am."
Suggested thought to contemplate: *"Now need I seek no more. LOVE has prevailed."*

Lesson 230 - "Now will I see and find the peace of God."
Suggested thought to contemplate: *"To remember God is Heaven."*

Lesson 231 - "Father, I will but to remember You."
Suggested thought to contemplate: *"God is here now, functioning perfectly."*

Lesson 232 - "Be in my mind, my Father, through the day."
Suggested thought to contemplate: *"I trust all things to God."*

Lesson 233 - "I give my life to God to guide today."
Suggested thought to contemplate: *"Be You the Guide, and I the follower."*

Lesson 234 - "Father, today I am Your Son again."
Suggested thought to contemplate: *"We thank you, Father, that we cannot lose the memory of You and of Your Love."*

Lesson 235 - "God in His mercy wills that I be saved."
Suggested thought to contemplate: *"I am safe forever in God's Arms."*

Lesson 236 - "I rule my mind, which I alone must rule."
Suggested thought to contemplate: *"Here I am, Father, listening for Your Voice."*

Lesson 237 - "Now would I be as God created me."
Suggested thought to contemplate: *"I behold the world that God would have me see."*

Lesson 238 - "On my decision all salvation rests."
Suggested thought to contemplate: *"I am beloved of God."*

Lesson 239 - "The glory of my Father is my own."
Suggested thought to contemplate: *"We thank you Father for the light that shines forever in us."*

Lesson 240 - "Fear is not justified in any form."
Suggested thought to contemplate: *"There is no fear in me, for I am part of Love Itself."*

Lesson 241 - "This holy instant is salvation come."
Suggested thought to contemplate: *"What joy there is today!"*

Lesson 242 - "This day is God's. It is my gift to Him" Suggested thought to contemplate: *"I will not lead my life alone today."*

Lesson 243 - "Today I will judge nothing that occurs."
Suggested thought to contemplate: *"Today, I am relieved of judgments that I cannot make."*

Lesson 244 - "I am in danger nowhere in the world."
Suggested thought to contemplate: *"I am secure in God."*

Lesson 245 - "Your peace is with me, Father. I am safe."
Suggested thought to contemplate: *"Your peace surrounds me, Father."*

Lesson 246 - "To love my Father is to Love His Son."
Suggested thought to contemplate: *"I will accept the way You choose for me to come to You, my Father."*

Lesson 247 - "Without forgiveness I will still be blind."
Suggested thought to contemplate: *"My brothers'/sisters' loveliness reflects my own."*

Lesson 248 - "Whatever suffers is not part of me."
Suggested thought to contemplate: *"Father, my ancient love for You returns."*

Lesson 249 - "Forgiveness ends all suffering and loss."
Suggested thought to contemplate: *"Father, we return our minds to you."*

Lesson 250 - "Let me not see myself as limited."
Suggested thought to contemplate: *"Today I would behold my Father's gentleness instead of my illusions."*

Lesson 251 - "I am in need of nothing but the truth."
Suggested thought to contemplate: *"For Your Peace, our Father, we give thanks."*

Lesson 252 - "The Son of God is my Identity."
Suggested thought to contemplate today: *"The Son of God may play he has become a body, prey to evil and to guilt, with but a little life that ends in death. But all the while his Father shines*

on him, and loves him with an everlasting Love which his pretenses cannot change at all."
This quote is from the *What is Sin* section that introduces these lessons. I know it is a bit longer than our usual thoughts but well worth the contemplation. Do you agree?

Lesson 253 - "My Self is ruler of the universe."
Suggested thought to contemplate: *"I surrender to my Real Self as ruler of my life."*

Lesson 254 - "Let every voice but God's be still in me."
Suggested thought to contemplate: *"Father, I come to You to ask You for the truth."*

Lesson 255 - "This day I choose to spend in perfect peace."
Suggested thought to contemplate: *"My Father, I pass this day with you."*

Lesson 256 - "God is the only goal I have today."
Suggested thought to contemplate today: *"The way to god is through forgiveness here. THERE IS NO OTHER WAY!"*

Lesson 257 - "Let me remember what my purpose is."
Suggested thought to contemplate: *"Father, forgiveness is Your chosen means to happiness."*

Lesson 258 - "Let me remember that my goal is God."
Suggested thought to contemplate: *"What could we want but to remember God?"*

Lesson 259 - "Let me remember that there is no sin."
Suggested thought to contemplate: *"Father, I would not be insane today. I would not be afraid of love."*

Lesson 260 - "Let me remember God created me."
Suggested thought to contemplate: *"Father, I call on you today. Let me remember You created me."*

Lesson 261 - "God is my refuge and security."
Suggested thought to contemplate: *"In God I find my refuge and my strength."*

Lesson 262 - "Let me perceive no differences today."
Suggested thought to contemplate: *"I speak only to God in each person today."*

Lesson 263 - "My holy vision sees all things as pure."
Suggested thought to contemplate: *"I look on all I see through holy vision and the eyes of Christ."*

Lesson 264 - "I am surrounded by the Love of God."
Suggested thought to contemplate: *"What surrounds me and keeps me safe is God's Love."*

Lesson 265 - "Creation's gentleness is all I see."
Suggested thought to contemplate: *"Today I see the world in celestial gentleness with which creation shines."*

Lesson 266 - "My holy Self abides in you, God's Son."
Suggested thought to contemplate: *"This day we enter into paradise, calling upon God's Name and on our own."*

Lesson 267 - "My heart is beating in the peace of God."
Suggested thought to contemplate: *"Each heartbeat brings me peace and each breath infuses me with strength."*

Lesson 268 - "Let all things be exactly as they are."
Suggested thought to contemplate: *"In Love was I created, and in Love will I remain forever."*

Lesson 269 - "My sight goes forth to look upon Christ's face."
Suggested thought to contemplate: *"Today, I choose to see the world forgiven, in which everyone shows me the face of Christ."*

Lesson 270 - "I will not use the body's eyes today."
Suggested thought to contemplate: *"The quiet of today will bless our hearts, and through them peace will come to everyone."*

Lesson 271 - "Christ's is the vision I will use today."
Suggested thought to contemplate: *"The Christ is God's Son as He created Him."*

Lesson 272 - "How can illusions satisfy God's Son?"
Suggested thought to contemplate: *"I am surrounded by Your*

Love, forever still, forever gentle and forever safe."

Lesson 273 - "The stillness of the peace of God is mine."
Suggested thought to contemplate: *"I cannot lose God's gifts to me."*

Lesson 274 - "Today belongs to Love. Let me not fear."
Suggested thought to contemplate: *"Father, today I would let all things be as you created them."*

Lesson 275 - "God's healing Voice protects all things today."
Suggested thought to contemplate: *"I need be anxious over nothing, for Your Voice will tell me all I need to know."*

Lesson 276 - "The Word of God is given me to speak."
Suggested thought to contemplate: *"Let me accept God's Fatherhood and all is given me."*

Lesson 277 - "Let me not bind Your Son with laws I made."
Suggested thought to contemplate: *"Let me not imagine I am bound by laws I made to rule the body."*

Lesson 278 - "If I am bound, my Father is not free."
Suggested thought to contemplate: *"Only love is sure."*

Lesson 279 - "Creation's freedom promises my own."
Suggested thought to contemplate: *"I accept God's promises and give my faith to them today."*

Lesson 280 - "What limits can I lay upon God's Son?"
Suggested thought to contemplate: *"Father, I lay no limits on the Son You love and You created limitless."*

Lesson 281 - "I can be hurt by nothing but my thoughts."
Suggested thought to contemplate: *"I will not hurt myself today."*

Lesson 282 - "I will not be afraid of love today."
Suggested thought to contemplate: *"Father, your Name is Love and so is mine. Such is the truth."*

Lesson 283 - "My true Identity abides in You."
Suggested thought to contemplate: *"Let me not worship idols. I am he my Father loves."*

Lesson 284 - "I can elect to change all thoughts that hurt."
Suggested thought to contemplate: *"Let me trust in God today, accepting but the joyous as His gifts, accepting but the joyous as the truth."*

Lesson 285 - "My holiness shines bright and clear today."
Suggested thought to contemplate: *"Father, I ask for only joyous things, the instant I accept my holiness."*

Lesson 286 - "The hush of Heaven holds my heart today."
Suggested thought to contemplate: *"In God has every conflict been resolved."*

Lesson 287 - "You are my goal, my Father. Only You."
Suggested thought to contemplate: *"What gift would I prefer before the peace of God."*

Lesson 288 - "Let me forget my brother's past today."
Suggested thought to contemplate: *"My brother's/sister's sins are in the past along with mine, and I am saved because the past is gone."*

Lesson 289 - "The past is over. It can touch me not."
Suggested thought to contemplate: *"I will wait no longer for the loveliness You have promised me."*

Lesson 290 - "My present happiness is all I see"
Suggested thought to contemplate: *"Father, I come to you and ask your strength to hold me up today, as I seek to do Your Will."*

Lesson 291 - "This is a day of stillness and of peace."
Suggested thought to contemplate: *"Father, I do not know the way to You. Guide me along the quiet path that leads to you."*

Lesson 292 - "A happy outcome to all things is sure."
Suggested thought to contemplate: *"God's promises make no exceptions and He guarantees happy endings."*

Lesson 293 – "All fear is past and only love is here."
Suggested thought to contemplate: *"I am willing to hear the hymns of gratitude the world is singing underneath the sounds of fear."*

Lesson 294 - "My body is a wholly neutral thing."
Suggested thought to contemplate: *"I am a Son of God. And can I be another thing as well?"*

Lesson 295 - "The Holy Spirit looks through me today."
Suggested thought to contemplate: *"Help me to use the eyes of Christ today, and thus allow The Holy Spirit's Love to bless all things."*

Lesson 296 - "The Holy Spirit speaks through me today."
Suggested thought to contemplate: *"I seek and find the easy path to God."*

Lesson 297 - "Forgiveness is the only gift I give."
Suggested thought to contemplate: *"Father, how certain are Your ways; how sure their final outcome."*

Lesson 298 - "I love You, Father, and I love Your Son."
Suggested thought to contemplate: *"All that would intrude upon my holy sight, forgiveness takes away."*

Lesson 299 - "Eternal holiness abides in me."
This is a most powerful lesson. If we could just get this message nothing would be denied us. Just think, ETERNAL holiness abides in me/you. Guilt about anything is nothing. Let's practice this thought whenever we feel guilty about anything. *"No matter what we do or don't do, ETERNAL holiness abides it us and there is nothing our holiness cannot do."*

Lesson 300 - "Only an instant does this world endure."
Suggested thought to contemplate: *"It is serenity we seek today, unclouded, obvious and sure."*

Lesson 301 - "And God Himself shall wipe away all tears."
Suggested thought to contemplate: *"We wept because we did not understand."*

Lesson 302 - "Where darkness was I look upon the light."
Suggested thought to contemplate: *"Our Love awaits us as we go to HIM, and walks beside us showing us the way."*

Lesson 303 - "The Holy Christ is born in me today."
Suggested thought to contemplate: *"I am safe in God's Arms."*

Lesson 304 - "Let not my world obscure the sight of Christ."
Suggested thought to contemplate: *"What I look on is my state of mind, reflected outward."*

Lesson 305 - "There is a peace that Christ bestows on us."
Suggested thought to contemplate: *"Love has come and healed the world by giving it Christ's peace."*

Lesson 306 - "The gift of Christ is all I seek today."
Suggested thought to contemplate: *"Father, we return to you, remembering we never went away, remembering Your holy gifts to us."*

Lesson 307 - "Conflicting wishes cannot be my will."
Suggested thought to contemplate: *"I am one with God in being and in will, and nothing contradicts the holy truth that I remain as God created me."*

Lesson 308 – "This instant is the only time there is."
Suggested thought to contemplate: *"I accept God's present blessing to the world, restoring it to timelessness and love."*

Lesson 309 - "I will not fear to look within today."
Suggested thought to contemplate: *"Within me is Eternal Innocence, because it is God's Will that it be there forever."*
Let's use this day to connect with our ETERNAL Innocence, no matter what is in our past. In this Now Moment we are Eternally Innocent. God is right and we have been wrong about ourselves.

Lesson 310 - "In fearlessness and love I spend today."
Suggested thought to contemplate: *"All the world joins with us in our song of thankfulness and joy to Him."*

Lesson 311 - "I judge all things as I would have them be."
Suggested thought to contemplate: *"God will relieve us of the*

agony of all the judgments we have made against ourselves."

Lesson 312 - "I see all things as I would have them be."
Suggested thought to contemplate: *"I have no purpose for today except to look upon a liberated world set free from all the judgments I have made."*

Lesson 313 - "Now let a new perception come to me."
Suggested thought to contemplate: *"How beautiful we are! How holy and how loving."*

Lesson 314 - "I seek a future different from the past."
Suggested thought to contemplate: *"Father, we were mistaken in the past, and choose to use the present to be free."*

Lesson 315 - "All gifts my brothers give belong to me."
Suggested thought to contemplate: *"Each day a thousand treasures come to me with every passing moment."*

Lesson 316 - "All gifts I give my brothers are my own."
Suggested thought to contemplate: *"My treasure house is full and angels watch its open doors that not one gift is lost and only more are added."* I have always loved this one!

Lesson 317 - "I follow in the way appointed me."
Suggested thought to contemplate: *"All my sorrows end in Your embrace."*

Lesson 318 - "In me, salvation's means and end are one."
Suggested thought to contemplate: *"I am God's Creation, His eternal Love."*

Lesson 319 - "I came for the salvation of the world."
Suggested thought to contemplate: *"It is the Will of God that what one gains is given unto all."*

Lesson 320 - "My Father gives all power unto me."
Suggested thought to contemplate: *"God's Will can do all things in me."*

Lesson 321 - "Father, my freedom is in You alone."
Suggested thought to contemplate: *"Father, Your Voice directs*

me, and the way to You is opening and clear to me at last."

Lesson 322 - "I can give up but what was never real."
Suggested thought to contemplate: *"What loss can I anticipate except the loss of fear, and the return of love into my mind?"*

Lesson 323 - "I gladly make the 'sacrifice' of fear."
Suggested thought to contemplate: *"I freely let love come streaming in to my awareness, healing me of pain, and giving me eternal joy."*

Lesson 324 - "I merely follow, for I would not lead."
Suggested thought to contemplate: *"Your loving Voice will always guide me aright."* I have always loved this one.

Lesson 325 - "All things I think I see reflect ideas."
Suggested thought to contemplate: *"From my forgiving thoughts, a gentle world comes forth."*

Lesson 326 - "I am forever an Effect of God."
Suggested thought to contemplate: *"God's Will be done on earth as we are restored to sanity, and to be as God created us."*

Lesson 327 - "I need but call and You will answer me.
Suggested thought to contemplate: *"Father, I thank you that Your promises will never fail in my experience, if I but test them out."*

Lesson 328 - "I choose the second place to gain the first."
Suggested thought to contemplate: *"I am glad that nothing I imagine contradicts what You would have me be."*

Lesson 329 - "I have already chosen what You will."
Suggested thought to contemplate: *"Father, my will is Yours. And I am safe, untroubled and serene, in endless joy, because it is Your Will that it be so.*

Lesson 330 - "I will not hurt myself again today."
Suggested thought to contemplate: *"Let me choose today that God be my Identity, and thus escape forever from all things the dream of fear appears to offer us."*

Lesson 331 - "There is no conflict, for my will is Yours."
Suggested thought to contemplate: *"You love me, Father."* Short and powerful.

Lesson 332 - "Fear binds the world. Forgiveness sets it free."
Suggested thought to contemplate: *"Thank you Father, that the Truth is true, and nothing else is true."*

Lesson 333 - "Forgiveness ends the dream of conflict here."
Suggested thought to contemplate: *"Father, forgiveness is the light You chose to shine away all conflict and all doubt, and light the way for our return to You."*

Lesson 334 - "Today I claim the gifts forgiveness gives."
Suggested thought to contemplate: *"One lily of forgiveness changes the darkness into light; the altar to illusion to the shrine of Life Itself. And peace will be restored forever to the holy minds which God created as His Son, His dwelling-place, His joy, His love, completely His, completely one with Him."* [68]

Lesson 335 - "I choose to see my brother's sinlessness."
Suggested thought to contemplate: *"Forgiveness is a choice."*

Lesson 336 - "Forgiveness lets me know that minds are joined."
Suggested thought to contemplate: *"God's Love is still abiding in my heart."*

Lesson 337 - "My sinlessness protects me from all harm."
Suggested thought to contemplate: *"I must learn I need do nothing of myself, for I need but accept my Self."*

Lesson 338 - "I am affected only by my thoughts."
Suggested thought to contemplate: *"I have the power to exchange each fear thought for a happy thought of love."*

Lesson 339 - "I will receive whatever I request."
Suggested thought to contemplate: *"Father, this is Your day. It is a day in which I would do nothing by myself, but hear Your Voice in everything I do."*

---

[68] W-330.12.5

Lesson 340 - "I can be free of suffering today." Suggested thought to contemplate: *"Be glad today! There is no room for anything but joy and thanks today."*

Lesson 341 - "I can attack but my own sinlessness, and it is only that which keeps me safe." Suggested thought to contemplate: *"How safe, how pure, how holy are we, abiding in God's smile."*

Lesson 342 - "I let forgiveness rest upon all things, for thus forgiveness will be given me." Suggested thought to contemplate: *"I let forgiveness rest upon all things today."*

Lesson 343 - "I am not asked to make a sacrifice to find the mercy and peace of God." Suggested thought to contemplate: *"The mercy and the peace of God are free and I accept this now."*

Lesson 344 - "Today I learn the law of love; that what I give my brother is my gift to me." Suggested thought to contemplate: *"How near we are to one another, as we go to God."*

Lesson 345 - "I offer only miracles today. For I would have them be returned to me." Suggested thought to contemplate: *"Peace to all seeking hearts today."*

Lesson 346 - "Today the peace of God envelops me, and I forget all things except His Love." Suggested thought to contemplate: *"I would forget all things except Your law of Love. I would abide in You, and know no laws except Your law of love."*

Lesson 347 - "Anger must come from judgment. Judgment is the weapon I would use against myself, To keep the miracle away from me." Suggested thought to contemplate: *"Be very still, and hear the gentle Voice for God assuring you that He has judged you as the Son He loves."*

Lesson 348 - "I have no cause for anger or for fear, for You surround me. And in every need that I perceive, Your grace suffices me." Suggested thought to contemplate: *"Father, let me remember You are here, and I am not alone."*

Lesson 349 - "Today I let Christ's vision look upon all things for me and judge them not, but give each one a miracle of love instead." Suggested thought to contemplate: *"Our Father knows our needs. He gives us grace to meet them all."*

Lesson 350 - "Miracles mirror God's eternal Love. To offer them is to remember Him, and through His memory to save the world." Suggested thought to contemplate: *"Father, only Your memory will set me free."*

Lesson 351 - "My sinless brother is my guide to peace. My sinful brother is my guide to pain. And which I choose to see I will behold." Suggested thought to contemplate: *"I see my sinlessness, my everlasting Comforter and Friend beside me and my way secure and clear."*

Lesson 352 - "Judgment and love are opposites. From one come all the sorrows of the world. But from the other comes the peace of God Himself." Suggested thought to contemplate: *"You have not left me comfortless."*

Lesson 353 - "My eyes, my tongue, my hands, my feet today have but one purpose; to be given Christ to use to bless the world with miracles." Suggested thought to contemplate: *"Father, I give all that is mine to Christ today."*

Lesson 354 - "We stand together, Christ and I, in peace and certainty of purpose. And in Him is His Creator, as He is in me." Suggested thought to contemplate: *"We stand together, Christ and I, in peace."*

Lesson 355 - "There is no end to all the peace and joy, and all the miracles that I will give, when I accept God's Word. Why not today?" Suggested thought to contemplate: *"Why should I wait, my Father, for the joy You promised me?"*

Lesson 356 - "Sickness is but another name for sin (missing the mark). Healing is but another name for God. The miracle is thus a call to Him." Suggested thought to contemplate: *"Healing is another name for God."*

Lesson 357 - "Truth answers every call we make to God. Responding first with miracles, and then returning unto us to be itself." Suggested thought to contemplate: *"Forgiveness, truth's reflection, tells me how to offer miracles, and thus escape the prison house in which I think I live."*

Lesson 358 - "No call to God can be unheard nor left unanswered. And of this I can be sure; His answer is the one I really want." Suggested thought to contemplate: *"Heavenly Father, let me not forget Your Love and care."*

Lesson 359 - "God's answer is some form of peace. All pain is healed; all misery replaced with joy. All prison doors are opened. And all sin is understood as merely a mistake." Suggested thought to contemplate: *"Father, today we will forgive Your world, and let creation be Your Own."*

Lesson 360 - "Peace be to me, the holy Son of God. Peace to my brother, who is one with me. Let all the world be blessed with peace through us." Suggested thought to contemplate: *"In holiness were we created, and in holiness do we remain."*

Lesson 361 - "This holy instant would I give to You. Be You in charge. For I would follow You, certain that Your direction gives me peace." Suggested thought to contemplate: *"If I need a word to help me, He will give it to me."*

Lesson 362 - "This holy instant would I give to You. Be You in charge. For I would follow You, certain that Your direction gives me peace." Suggested thought to contemplate, from the Epilogue: *"Your Friend (the Holy Spirit) goes with you. You are not alone."*

Lesson 363 - "This holy instant would I give to You. Be You in charge. For I would follow You, certain that Your direction gives me peace." Suggested thought to contemplate, from the Epilogue: *"No one who calls on Him can call in vain. Whatever troubles you, be certain that He has the answer, and will gladly give it to you."*

Lesson 364 - "This holy instant would I give to You. Be You in charge. For I would follow You, certain that Your direction gives me peace." Suggested thought to contemplate, from the Epilogue: *"You are as certain of arriving home as is the pathway of the sun laid down before it rises, after it has set, and in the half lit hours in between. Indeed, your pathway is more certain still."*

Lesson 365 - "This holy instant would I give to You. Be You in charge. For I would follow You, certain that Your direction gives me peace." Suggested thought to contemplate, from the Epilogue:

"We trust our ways to Him and say 'Amen'. In peace we will continue in His way, and trust all things to Him. In confidence we wait His answers, as we ask His Will in everything we do. He loves God's Son as we would love him. And He teaches us how to behold him through His eyes and love him as He does. You do not walk alone. God's angels hover near and all about. His Love surrounds you, and of this be sure; that I will never leave you comfortless."

May the coming years be filled with the awareness of the Love of God for you and yours.

Mary Barbara

About the Author

Mary Barbara Jankowski is tops on my Most Memorable People list. She is one of those rare individuals who you feel lucky to have known. We first met about two decades ago and I am still captivated by her zest to keep *love, laughter and forgiveness* as her focus in her personal life and while facilitating "A Course in Miracles" (the Course) groups.

Mary started facilitating groups in the Course in 1983. In addition to facilitating up to four groups weekly, she has counseled countless individuals. Her emphasis has always been to guide students to apply the principles expressed in the Course to all aspects of their lives.

She takes the firm stance that the Course *is* the absolute truth in her life and shares that philosophy with everyone who is fortunate enough to know her or attend one of her groups.

Despite experiencing trials and tribulations in her personal life during her time here in *Earth School*, she continues to grow and teach all whom she encounters. As her dear friend, I'd like to say *thank you Mary,* for helping me and countless others become enlightened and encouraged as a result of your uncompromising love and forgiveness.

Irene Murphy

Product Information:
A Path To Peace is marketed through Amazon.com

Made in United States
Orlando, FL
07 February 2025

58268762R00098